Stewart Z offe 72

PELICAN BOOK A963

British Institutions
Advisory Editor: J. H. Plumb

THE JUSTICE OF THE PEACE

Esther Moir was brought up in the Welsh borders. She read history at Cambridge and then did research on the Justices of the Peace in Gloucestershire in the eighteenth century for a Cambridge Ph.D.

She was attached to the Department of English Local History at Leicester University for two years, and worked in London before returning to Cambridge to teach modern history at Newnham College.

In 1964 she published *The Discovery of Britain: The English Tourists 1540–1840*, and her work on the Gloucestershire Justices is shortly to appear as a book.

She now teaches part-time in the Department of Economic History at Nottingham University. She is married to the Rev. Victor de Waal, and they have four small sons.

BRITISH INSTITUTIONS

*

THE JUSTICE
OF THE PEACE

ESTHER MOIR

PENGUIN BOOKS

Penguin Books Ltd, Harmondsworth, Middlesex, England
Penguin Books Inc., 7110 Ambassador Road, Baltimore, Maryland 21207, U.S.A.
Penguin Books Australia Ltd, Ringwood, Victoria, Australia

—

First published 1969

—

Copyright © Esther Moir, 1969

—

Made and printed in Great Britain by
Richard Clay (The Chaucer Press), Ltd
Bungay, Suffolk
Set in Monotype Times

TO
JOHN, ALEXANDER, EDMUND
AND THOMAS

CONTENTS

INTRODUCTION

'CERTAINLY to anyone who has an eye for historical greatness it is a very marvellous institution, this Commission of the Peace, growing so steadily, elaborating itself into ever new forms,' wrote F. W. Maitland, the great nineteenth-century legal historian, and then he added, 'it is so purely English, perhaps the most distinctively English part of all our governmental organization.'[1]* There is indeed something extraordinary about an office held by unpaid amateurs throughout six centuries of English history which has become so deeply embedded in national life that even today, though its form may be discussed, the value of its continued existence is rarely questioned. Purely English though it may have been in origin, it has nevertheless been extended first to Wales, Scotland and Ireland, making an important contribution to the unity of the institutional and legal history of Great Britain, and has subsequently been adopted by the Commonwealth. 'The whole Christian world hath not the like office as justice of the peace if duly executed,' wrote Sir Edward Coke in the early seventeenth century. It is unique: sometimes one is tempted to say also that it is impossible. For the great majority of people for the greater part of this country's history the government in London was something remote, almost irrelevant to their lives. The reality of government lay with their local Justice of the Peace, who, whether individually in his own front parlour, with a neighbour at some nearby inn, or with the whole county gathered in Quarter Sessions, determined matters of life and death, saw to the maintenance of such rudimentary public services as roads and bridges, and supervised the elementary beginnings of public welfare in the care of the aged, poverty-stricken and illegitimate. In the first instance these men were just what their title implies, guardians of the peace, responsible for the maintenance of law and order, whether that meant dealing with the riotous elements of the population in the fourteenth century or with the Chartist uprisings of the 1840s. But this,

* References are listed on page 13.

though historically the basis of their duties, soon became overlaid, mainly in the sixteenth century, by a succession of tasks which in effect made them the pivot of all government in the locality, and more and more statutes were heaped upon their shoulders by a King and Council which recognized in them an army of executive officers ready made to serve the state.

But the J.P. was more than a servant of the state, his duties designated by statute, his functions institutional ones. He was also the pivotal point of local life in all its aspects at a time when the neighbourhood and its affairs mattered far more to the inhabitants of this country than organs of central government in Whitehall or Westminster. Something which is made very clear by a study of the J.P. through the centuries is the extent to which England was essentially local, both in feeling and in organization, right up to the last century. A man thought of himself as belonging to his native county and this was something which meant a very great deal to him. Generation after generation of a landed family would serve the county in which their acres lay. County knowledge, relationships, loyalties, feuds, were the stuff of life, considerably more real than any wider commitment. The picture which emerges from an investigation of the Justices in the years immediately preceding the Civil War shows the England of 1640 resembling a 'union of partially independent shire-states, each with its own distinct ethos and loyalty'.[2] The lesson which the Cromwellian regime taught the country was that county gentry must be employed to govern their local counties: this was the natural order of things and to flout it was to court disaster. For while the patriarchal ideals of a landed society were widely accepted – and they were so tenacious and resilient under pressure of change that even in the nineteenth century they were still able to resist the challenge presented by the values of the new urbanized and industrial society – the great strength of the J.P. lay in the *natural* foundation of his power. The central government might create an office by statute and might endow it with an ever increasing number of duties. But the authority which the Justice commanded, and which those below him recognized, can never be understood in purely institutional terms. The local man who knew, and, more important, understood his locality, linked by countless ties of blood and friendship to other men of similar circumstances in the same county, was inevitably involved in local affairs to a degree which could never have been formally created by any Act of Parliament. It is no exaggeration to say that a dimension is lost in understanding the history of this country in all its aspects, social, political, constitutional, if the Justice of the Peace is not brought firmly into the picture. This local ruler is no mere Squire Western, a bucolic figure to be hastily dismissed by those concerned with matters of greater moment. If local life is of significance in England's development so is that local figure *par excellence*, the Justice of the Peace.

The history of the office of Justice of the Peace should be of interest not only to the historian but to lawyers, sociologists and also, one would hope, to those who hold that office today. It is therefore all the more surprising that so little attention has been paid to it. At the end of the nineteenth century, in the years following the County Council Act of 1888 which saw the radical transformation of the office, there was a considerable amount of interest in and writing on the subject – by Maitland, by Josef Redlich and Francis Hirst in 1903, and of course by Sidney and Beatrice Webb, the first volume of whose magnificent *English Local Government* appeared in 1906. But inevitably they all wrote within the limitations of their age, and their preconceptions, even, in the case of the Webbs, their political bias, have dated and to some extent limited the usefulness of their scholarship. The Webbs, for example, true Fabians and reformers that they were were most unwilling to admit that government based upon a landowning interest and reflecting aristocratic leadership (in its widest sense) could govern this country and could govern it well throughout the eighteenth century.

Since the appearance early in this century of these great general studies the main contribution to our knowledge of the history of local government has come from the publication by individual counties of Quarter Sessions records, in editions which vary both in quality and usefulness. Usually an introduction which describes the machinery of Quarter Sessions and its hierarchy of officials is followed by extracts from the sessions rolls, a tedious succession of court orders on bastardy, licensing, highways, the Poor

11

Law. These are the raw materials of history certainly, but their painstaking editors do not pause to consider that in every county the forms of the machinery were the same but the men who controlled it were different, and it is about *them* that we really want to know. Who were the Justices of the Peace? What use did they make of the powers that they enjoyed? They could, after all, make a mockery of the statutes passed at Westminster. If they were so inclined a statute might be well and methodically executed, but if they disliked it it would remain a dead letter, its clauses never implemented, its intentions no more than an empty gesture on the part of those men who, in the Privy Council or in the Houses of Parliament, might like to think they held the reins of power securely in their hands, but who, in the last resort, depended to a degree they were probably unwilling to recognize, upon the cooperation of scores of country squires.

At a time when the office of Justice of the Peace is again under review, when the appointment, training and payment of the magistracy is being discussed and thought out afresh, it may be an opportune moment to look at the development of the institution in the past. We are in a better position today than were the Webbs to make a full and objective assessment of the office, for historical scholarship has changed much in the sixty years since they wrote. Sir John Neale and Sir Lewis Namier, in their work on the House of Commons in the sixteenth and eighteenth centuries respectively, have given models of the sort of analysis of personnel which is necessary if we are to discover the flesh and blood which underlie such general terms as M.P. or J.P. The recent emphasis on the importance of economic history makes it difficult to take the political institutions of the country as a subject for study out of their social and economic context and it has become clear that the varying character of the Benches must be seen as a reflection of the agrarian and industrial development of the individual counties. The advances made in local history have destroyed for ever the hope that one could write the history of local government as a unified system throughout the country: we have come to recognize that we shall be much nearer the truth if we think of England as made up of vigorous and self-conscious regions until at least the nineteenth century.

Miss Bertha Putnam, the great authority on the medieval Justices, apologized to her readers that 'for so wide a range of investigation the thirty years of research devoted to the justices of the peace have proved all too few'.[3] This work claims to be no more than a general survey, a synthesis as far as possible of recent writing on the subject at both the local and the national level. The chapters concerning the eighteenth century do however contain a certain amount of original material based on my thesis *The Justices of the Peace in Gloucestershire 1775–1800*,[4] and I am most grateful to Mr Irvine Gray and the staff of the Gloucestershire County Record Office for their unstinting help during the time when I was working in the county. Miss Olive Lloyd-Baker of Hardwick Court, Gloucestershire, very kindly allowed me to see the family papers and I should like to express my thanks to her. The chapter on the medieval period has benefited from the advice of Dr R. L. Storey; the chapters on the sixteenth and seventeenth centuries from the help of Dr M. C. Cross and Dr A. M. Everitt. I am grateful to Professor J. H. Plumb for his encouragement and criticism throughout.

Nottingham
July 1967

References

1. *Collected Papers*, ed. H. A. L. Fisher, Cambridge University Press, 1911, II, p. 470.
2. A. M. Everitt, 'Social Mobility in Early Modern England', *Past and Present*, 1966, No. 33, p. 59.
3. *Proceedings before the Justices of the Peace in the Fourteenth and Fifteenth Centuries, Edward III to Richard III*, Ames Foundation Publication, Cambridge, Massachusetts, 1938, p. xiv.
4. *Local Government in Gloucestershire, 1775–1800, A Study of the Justices of the Peace*, Bristol and Gloucestershire Archaeological Society Records Series, 1969.

CHAPTER ONE

1300–1485
Medieval Origins

IT was under the threat of a mounting crime wave – a situation
which the mid twentieth century will recognize with sympathy –
that the Justices of the Peace were instituted in the fourteenth
century, in an attempt to strengthen the already existing forces of
law and order. The mechanism by which the elements at least of
good order were imposed upon medieval society were complex,
far more complex than any straightforward description of the
judicial system of the time could ever convey. Rules of custom
and of religion played their part as well as rules of law. But the
influence of the moral code and the authority of tradition and
custom are less easy to discover than the rules which were imposed by force. The sources available to the historian do not
make up a full picture: official records tell of the proceedings of
the courts, particularly at the highest level, but the lack of diaries,
letters and other private and personal material means that the
influences which moulded and guided men's attitudes are difficult
to assess. The obligations which bound man to man, the regard
in which the Church's teaching was held, the respect due to the
local landowner from those below him in the social scale – all
the social conventions in fact which determined behaviour – on
these the evidence is lacking. Our view is therefore built up
mainly from the records of the courts, the royal courts presided
over by judges appointed by the royal government, and the local
courts of the county, hundred (that is, a division within a county),
borough or manor, which, though they administered the law of
the land, were nearly all privately controlled.[1]

The judicial system at this stage in its evolution is impressive. At
its apex were the King, the Privy Council and Parliament. Below
came the three great central courts: the court of common pleas

which heard cases between subject and subject, and corrected the errors in the local courts; the court of King's Bench which handled cases of special concern to the King; and the Exchequer, which has been well called the 'Local Government Board of medieval England',[2] to which was rendered the account of finances collected on behalf of the Crown and which entertained cases arising from the audit of the revenue. In addition the justices of these superior courts made regular tours of the country and brought the central courts into direct touch with the local populace.

The records of such courts tell of the violence and tensions within society. In medieval England the possibility, indeed the general likelihood, of riot and rebellion, was never far distant. Hardly a generation passed without some major disturbance, and every village was only too familiar with the brawls and petty violence of daily life. 'The internal peace of the kingdom was poised on a razor's edge.'[3] On the national level a key factor was the person of the King. A strong ruler had some prospect of fulfilling the promises made in his coronation oath, but it was little more than an empty hope that a weak monarch could maintain effective government and preserve peace and justice. The centralized judicial system with its network of royal officials throughout the country made good government possible, in that it could prevent or if necessary suppress public disorder, provided that the Crown was in a position to exploit it fully.

In the early years of the fourteenth century, when the incompetent and unpopular Edward II was on the throne, the country was threatened with widespread violence. The government was trying at this time to supplement the jurisdiction exercised in the courts by making use of other agencies, particularly of temporary commissions issued for specific purposes to specially appointed officials. One such commission was issued to the keepers of the peace. It was an attempt to harness the forces both of law and of custom, for the men designated to execute the law were the local knights and gentry, those who might be expected to command respect in their localities. They were described in an Act of 1327 (which did not in fact create the office but merely gave statutory sanction to an already established system) as 'bones gentz et leux . . . a la garde de la pees'. They were given authority to arrest suspects and to inquire into felonies and trespasses. But their position was a weak one in that they might only initiate proceedings but not determine them; they might inquire into offences but not punish them. Their lack of authority for any final process brought them little prestige compared with other peace-keeping bodies and also, more seriously, discouraged effective cooperation from other local officials, particularly from the Sheriff, the chief official in the shire, whose goodwill was necessary if they were to be able to work efficiently. Miss Putnam indeed has concluded that the organization and powers of the keepers of the peace at this date seem 'singularly futile',[4] and that if they were to be at all effective they had either to be demoted and given the status of constables of the hundreds, lesser men responsible for keeping the peace within these smaller divisions of the counties, or else have their authority increased to the extent of being allowed to determine their own indictments.

For some years in the middle of the fourteenth century it was by no means clear which way the pendulum would swing, and the whole future of the J.P.s hung in the balance. For whether the keepers of the peace should survive or not raised important issues concerning the most effective methods of preserving the peace of the realm. Opinion on this was quite clearly divided by the time of Edward III. On the one hand members of the central government, notably Sir Geoffrey Scrope, then Chief Justice of the King's Bench, wanted to rely on specially commissioned royal justices, probably distinguished lawyers and magnates, with extraordinary powers to deal with all offences. This he regarded not only as the best but also the most profitable means of restoring order since its proceedings would result in heavy financial exactions, a rich harvest of fines laid either on individuals or on whole districts, which would naturally be popular with a government chronically in urgent need of money. 'Profits of justice, not justice, were the essential consideration,' comments Miss Putnam drily.[5] But on the other hand the House of Commons, representing the interests of the gentry and burgesses, kept on urging the claims of commissions issued to the country gentry: in 1340–41 they were particularly vociferous in demanding that they should be given to men with some knowledge of local conditions.

For thirty years the powers entrusted to the keepers fluctuated according to the pressure exercised at Westminster. Some years saw their partial eclipse, others the restoration and extension of their authority. The greatest step forward came with the statute of 1361 (which has often though erroneously been taken as marking the origin of the office) which marked their transformation from keepers to Justices of the Peace by the official and permanent extension of their powers, giving them definite authority to determine felonies and trespasses. After this their progress still continued at an uncertain pace, but except for two very brief periods, between 1364 and 1368, and from 1382 to 1389, when the government turned once more to special emergency commissions, they never lost their power to determine the indictments they initiated. Moreover, their authority was gradually extended beyond criminal matters to cover economic and administrative affairs – again developments of the greatest significance for the future of the office which should by no means be taken for granted since they represent the success of pressure brought to bear upon the government by the House of Commons. For it was the Commons who particularly urged that the Justices should be given the execution of the mass of economic legislation which reached the statute book in the years succeeding the Black Death, when the plague brought home the fact that economic problems might be of as vital importance to the country as questions of peace and order.

The tenacity with which the Commons consistently advocated the extension of the powers of the J.P.s during these years is remarkable. From Miss Putnam's study of the parliamentary material of the period it is clear that time and time again a special request for the increase of their authority would be categorically refused, or a Commons petition would be granted in every respect except in regard to Justices. Often they succeeded only after repeating a demand in several Parliaments; sometimes they failed to achieve what they wanted for several generations. For example, petitions that the Justices should be allowed to deal with purveyance (that is, the right of the Crown to provisions or the use of horses at fixed price) were made in the time of Edward III and repeated under Richard II, Henry V and Henry VI, but only finally granted in full by a statute of 1441–2.[6] It is tempting to speculate upon the fate of English local government had the Justices remained what the government had first intended them to be, solely keepers of the peace, and had the Commons lost their battle to increase their authority and to add to it the execution of this growing volume of other legislation. Can it be said that the existence of the Justices has prevented the growth in England of a permanent bureaucracy such as took place for example in France?

English local government at the end of the Middle Ages was still a mosaic of different authorities, and the introduction of the J.P.s added yet one more complication to an already sufficiently confusing pattern of courts and officials. By the fifteenth century the Justices were beginning to show themselves serious rivals to some of the older shire officials. The authority of the Sheriff, who had earlier been the most important official in the shire, was already waning, and the coroner, his deputy, also found himself being made less and less use of by the Crown. An Act of 1461 sealed the supremacy of the J.P.s over the Sheriff when it laid down that all indictments and presentments which were normally taken at his tourn, when twice a year he presided over a sessions of each hundred in his shire and exercised summary jurisdiction over such petty offences as brawls and affrays, should in future be taken before the Justices. This was no mean victory, for the Sheriff who was appointed by the King and Council as the royal representative in the shires was able to exercise his influence in countless ways upon the conduct of county affairs. The Act was yet another triumph for the Commons. Indeed if between 1327 and 1485 the J.P.s acquire a firm status and clearly defined powers, this is largely due to the activity of the Commons on their behalf. It was an alliance from which both parties were to benefit much in the future.

It was perhaps only natural that the country gentry and the urban middle classes should encourage the growth of an office which was largely filled by members of their own class. For the commission of the peace, the corporate body of Justices, had soon established the social composition it was to maintain more or less unaltered for the succeeding five centuries. Each Bench of Justices contained a number of lay magnates but it consisted essentially of country gentry with a sprinkling of lawyers. The Commons phrased their demands in the most general of terms, 'bones gentz et loialx', though in one respect they made more specific requests, asking repeatedly that Justices should be men resident in their shires with some knowledge of local conditions. They were especially opposed to the practice of appointing famous lawyers to a number of commissions so that in fact business was done by deputies. It soon became clear that the phrase used in 1414, 'des plus sufficaunz', was too vague a description of men who would be suitably qualified and this was therefore amended in 1439 to a definite demand that all J.P.s should be holders of land worth £20 per annum freehold.

Although the central government technically appointed and to a large extent controlled the Justices, their selection was subject to local influence and reflected local interests. The extent of this influence and its exercise was in dispute during the fourteenth century when the Commons' petitions urged either some form of local election or nomination, or parliamentary control 'par l'advis des Seignurs et Communes de Parlement'. By the end of the century the petitions cease, and it seems that the theory of central control had been accepted. In practice however since this control was exercised through the Council and since it was customary to issue a new list of Justices almost every year, various channels of influence remained open to the Commons, and local committees continued to petition and to bring pressure to bear in Parliament.

The numbers on the commission in the early fourteenth century were small: no more than four or five men to each county. In 1338 Somerset for example had four Justices; in 1362 Staffordshire and Suffolk had three. An Act of 1388 provided for six Justices in every county, and this was raised to eight in 1390. As the popularity and authority of the office grew, numbers continued to increase until by the later fifteenth century it was usual to have twenty or so in the more populous counties. Every man named in the commission had to take an oath before he could serve, and his tenure of office then lasted until the issue of a new commission. A Clerk of the Peace to the Bench (as distinct from the personal clerk to an individual lawyer, from whose services the other Justices would naturally benefit) is first definitely mentioned in 1380 when the Justices were instructed to administer an oath to their clerk 'to conceal the counsel of the King and to perform his duties loyally'. These men often held office for periods of ten or fifteen years, and their main duties consisted of making up and keeping the records.[7] The matter of wages was finally settled in 1388 and 1390 at a rate of four shillings a day for Justices and two shillings a day for the Clerk of the Peace, up to a maximum of twelve days a year, for attendance at Quarter Sessions only.[8] Other duties – and they could be many – went unpaid, and Justices who were peers were not to receive wages.

Four times a year the medieval J.P. would sit with his fellow Justices in general Quarter Sessions for his native shire. The court when fully assembled, with the Bench of Justices, the juries, the local officials, clerks and prisoners, would have numbered a hundred or more, and the housing of such an assembly must have created something of a problem. In a number of places the castle would be the obvious place; Quarter Sessions certainly met in the castles at York, Winchester, Canterbury and Worcester. But when, as was often the case, sessions were not held at the principal town of any county, the local inn must have provided a less glorious setting. In a number of the larger counties, such as Yorkshire or Norfolk, sessions were held at what must have been little more than small towns or even large villages, places such as Pocklington or Kilham. Miss Putnam has found a striking example of this in the June sessions of 1361 for the North Riding, which were held in six different towns in eight days and must have involved the Justices and the court officials in some uncomfortably quick riding to cover the ground in time with all their paraphernalia of rolls and writs.[9] In a well-organized sessions, like that at Winchester which lasted three days, the first day would often be spent in a preliminary general sessions before several Justices, during which a proclamation might be made of recent statutes and a charge read to the group of jurors and officials standing in the body of the hall. Then the hearing of presentments and the trial of cases would follow on the succeeding days. A case would only be tried on the day following an indictment, often not until the following sessions. The notorious case in Warwickshire in which the Duke of Clarence, sitting as a Justice, managed to have an unfortunate woman indicted, tried, convicted and hanged all at one continuous sessions on the same day led to a vigorous protest from Parliament.[10]

The cases which were brought before the Justices in Quarter Sessions have the recurrent theme of violence, a violence moreover which was not limited to the peasantry and the lower orders, for the indictments on the sessions rolls tell of crimes committed by knights, canons, chaplains, local officials, even by the Justices themselves. The splendid chivalry of the nobility as Froissart describes it and the constant succession of bloody assaults and unedifying affrays which we hear of in the courts seem to belong to two different worlds. Equally, the traditions of medieval piety and of the worship and learning of medieval Christendom seem far removed from the evidence of violent scenes in church during Mass and of the great number of offences committed by ecclesiastics. The offices of law-enforcement created by the monarchy make impressive reading, but the sessions rolls reveal the other side of the picture: graft, favouritism, officials convicted of the very offences they were supposed to be preventing. Riots were by no means unknown at Quarter Sessions itself. Jurors were attacked, even in the presence of Justices, and sessions completely broken up. At Huntingdon on one occasion armed rioters with ladders tried to break into a room where the Justices were preparing for Quarter Sessions and set fire to it; at Bedford the Justices once gathered for the sessions already divided into two hostile groups, each with armed followers.

Indictments for assault and wounding were almost routine matters at Quarter Sessions and appear in the records with monotonous frequency. There are countless charges of being disorderly, disreputable or criminal persons, particularly at times of markets and fairs. There are occasional glimpses of a sinister underworld at which we can only guess, peopled by

22

gamesters, frequenters of taverns, players of games like 'peny-prik', 'sleepers by day and watchers by night who eat well and drink well – yet have nothing'.[11] Arson, rape and robbery are common, felonious housebreaking and homicide occur often. But the wide range of the Justices' peace-keeping activities can only be fully appreciated from examples of miscellaneous cases appearing before them: cutting down a hanged woman before she was dead; diverting a watercourse; killing a dog; removing a corpse from church; keeping a large portion of a tree near a highway in which robbers could rest; rousing the town against the constable of the castle. Economic offences increase, as time goes on, to make the list even longer, and the Justices found themselves dealing with forestallers, who bought up grain in order to force up the market price and sell it again at profit; brewers using illicit measures; middlemen buying by illegal weight; workers breaking contracts, taking excess wages and refusing to work under lawful conditions. At one moment, it is true, the Justices might be faced by a local peasant accused of taking swans or fish or changing the brand on a horse. But the next they might have to deal with a man like William Swanlund of York, one of the greatest financiers of the realm, a large-scale wool exporter who in the early 1360s had to be brought to book for buying wool by illegal weight in Yorkshire. The body of the Justices' work lay between these extremes, and its real value was in their day to day dealing with felonies and trespasses (often by exercising their powers of binding over to keep the peace) and with all the types of violence that so threatened public peace because they involved all ranks within society, officials of the realm as much as private persons.

With all their shortcomings (and it was not unknown for a Justice to draw his dagger at Quarter Sessions) by the end of the Middle Ages the Justices of the Peace had fully borne out the faith of the Commons that they offered the best potential means for keeping the peace. It is also apparent that the monarchy recognized this and was ready to lay new duties upon them. It would be too cynical to say that the Crown approved of them particularly because they were cheap, though this was of course true. They were also clearly the most satisfactory means of organizing local government. For to entrust such powers to the magnates would have been to weaken the throne, possibly to encourage civil war; to rely on officials like the Sheriff who depended on fees and tax-farming for a livelihood would have opened the way to corruption and oppression; while to appoint salaried officers was simply out of the question because there was no money to do so. But even so the advantages of the Justices were more than the negative ones of preventing the development in this country of an official class of local administrators, open to all the abuses which a permanent and salaried bureaucracy carries with it. The Justices remained essentially part of their local community, which has meant an interdependence between local government and the vitality of the county. Local government in this country has been strengthened even more by the fact that the Justices performed their functions under judicial forms and that, subject to the law, they enjoyed a large measure of autonomy. On the one hand this offered protection to the individual, on the other it encouraged the initiative and responsibility of that class of men who recognized their first duty as that of unpaid obligation to their immediate local community and who were prepared to translate that obligation into terms in which they could serve the state – and at the same time promote or at least safeguard their own interests.

References

1. This paragraph owes much to the suggestions made by R. H. Hilton in 'A Medieval Society', *The West Midlands at the End of the Thirteenth Century*, Weidenfeld & Nicolson, 1966, p. 217.
2. H. M. Cam, 'Shire Officials: Coroners, Constables, and Bailiffs', in *English Government at Work 1327–1336*, eds. J. F. Willard, W. A. Morris and W. H. Dunham, Medieval Academy of America, Cambridge, Massachusetts, 1950, III, p. 146.
3. R. L. Storey, *The End of the House of Lancaster*, Barrie & Rockcliff, 1966, p. 13.
4. B. Putnam, 'Shire Officials: Keepers of the Peace and Justices of the Peace', in *English Government at Work*, op. cit., p. 215.
5. B. Putnam, *Proceedings before the Justices of the Peace in the Fourteenth and Fifteenth Centuries, Edward III to Richard III*, 1938, p. xli.
6. *ibid.*, p. liii.
7. See H. C. Johnson, *The Origin and Office of the Clerk of the Peace*, reprint from *The Clerks of the Counties 1360–1960*, ed. Stephens, Society of Clerks, Shire Hall, Warwick, 1961.

8. Payment was of course customary to members of commissions with extraordinary powers; those enforcing the labour laws of 1349–51 for example had received five or six shillings a day for sitting up to a maximum of forty days a year. Putnam, *Proceedings*, p. lxxxix.

9. *Yorkshire Sessions of the Peace 1361–1364*, Yorkshire Archaeological Society, Record Series, Wakefield, 1939, p. xxi.

10. Putnam, *Proceedings*, p. civ.

11. *ibid.*, p. cxviii.

CHAPTER TWO

1485–1603
The Justice Comes of Age

As late as 1559 Lord Wharton still found 'Pleasure in acts d'armys' a fitting motto to inscribe upon his new gatehouse at Wharton Hall.[1] For centuries he and his fellow members of the aristocracy had been trained for a life of violence and the tradition died hard: the endemic disorder inherent in medieval society bred warlike men and a warlike set of values which did not disappear overnight. The Tudor triumph was to establish a royal monopoly over violence, an achievement which, as Professor Stone says, profoundly altered both the nature of politics and the quality of daily life. But it is all too easy to take this achievement for granted – particularly since the older textbooks, by dating the beginning of modern England to 1485, seem to imply that law and order were restored to the country from the reign of Henry VII.

Contemporaries had much to say of order, stability and degree, and to read the poets, philosophers and statesmen of the sixteenth century one would gain the impression that they knew and cherished an ordered society. All were agreed that as the world depended upon one great chain of being, so did the classes within the nation and the members within the family.[2] Hierarchy, and obedience to that hierarchy, were the twin pillars upon which all peace and stability rested. The classic statement of this orthodox view comes of course in *Troilus and Cressida*, and although by now somewhat hackneyed, it is still a valuable indication of what Shakespeare's world understood by 'degree'.

> O when degree is shak'd
> Which is the ladder to all high designs
> The enterprise is sick. How could communities.
> Degrees in schools, and brotherhoods in cities,

Peaceful commerce from dividable shores,
The primogenitye and due of birth,
Prerogative of age, crowns, sceptres, laurels
But by degree stand in authentic place?
Take but degree away, untune that string,
And hark, what discord follows.

But characteristically such sentiments are hymned most loudly at the very time when they are being challenged, are even breaking down. Analogies from astronomy and anatomy might seem to confirm the impregnable nature of stability; the Reformation might be presented as a return to the early church; new men might cloak their rising family fortunes with genealogies of Roman and Saxon provenance – but in fact change, insecurity and unrest were close to the surface, more of an ever-present reality to sixteenth-century society than its members allowed themselves to confess. The nobility did not easily give up their castles, their armouries and retainers; the lawlessness which permeated every rank of society below them died hard. Still throughout the 1570s and 1580s the greater nobles were drawing into their households 'gentlemen & esquiers of remarkable families and discent'; the Earl of Southampton was attended by one hundred gentlemen with golden chains about their necks, and the Earl of Oxford could ride into London at the head of eighty liveried gentlemen.[3] When Kenilworth was modernized by the Earl of Leicester in the 1570s it was also heavily fortified, and the nobility continued to accumulate munitions of enormous quantity and power, not merely firearms but cannon produced by the flourishing Wealdon iron industry. A gentleman went about armed, and had little hesitation in drawing sword upon slight provocation. Private animosity and quarrels ran throughout society, and if the nobility acted without restraint even more so did their retainers, who were frequently little better than hired ruffians and recognized no conventions about fair play in the feuds which sometimes amounted to local warfare.

It is hardly surprising then that in many parts of the country a restless insecurity prevailed throughout the sixteenth century. In the north and in Wales it was particularly serious, and as late as 1607 the President of the Council of Wales reported that violence was still widespread and blood-money and the blood-feud common. But elsewhere, even in the more settled midlands and home counties, local tyrannies and feuds not only disrupted the peace of landed society but created an atmosphere which encouraged crime and riot among the poor, the landless and the homeless. The hungry mouths and uncertain livelihood of the poor were enough excuse for their outrages in times of rising prices, enclosure and sharp economic fluctuations. Riots, brawls, assaults, murder, private feud, local faction: it is against this background that the Justice was called to the commission of the *peace*, and his foremost duty remained that of enforcing the royal statutes to maintain law and order. The Tudor struggle to combat the worst excesses of lawlessness was slow, cautious and not altogether successful. If by the end of the century violence had been brought within tolerable limits this was due in no small measure to the work of the Justices. What then do we know of the Justice of the Peace in the sixteenth century, and of his qualifications to act as the instrument of the Tudor monarchy in this formidable and unenviable undertaking?

The actual qualifications necessary for a Justice remained few and simple, for those inherited from previous reigns were perpetuated with little emendation. The demand that he should be worth £20 a year in land or tenements (18 Hen. VI c. 11) was now construed, since the value of money fell rapidly in the sixteenth century, as meaning that his status should be that of a country gentleman; and there was now, for the first time, specific reference to his religious convictions, since it was essential that he should adhere to the official forms of worship decreed by the state. The tests of suitability for office laid down by Elizabeth towards the end of her reign in fact amounted to little more than a restatement of the long familiar requirements, that a man should live in the county, be of sufficient living and countenance, be neither unlearned nor ignorant. She put the matter more succinctly in 1599 when she told the Chancellor to remove 'those that be drones and not bees'.[4]

The commission of the peace under which the Lord Chancellor appointed the Justices was not issued all at one time for the whole country, but when and where it was necessary to add or subtract names in any particular county. The usual view is that the number of Justices for any one county was settled by the Lord Chancellor acting upon nominations made by the Judges of Assize, but it seems much more likely, in the light of what we know of Elizabethan political practice in general, that the initiative came from the counties and reflects local influence, intrigue, even outright bribery. This may help to explain the curiously great difference in numbers between Essex with sixty-two Justices in 1561 and Kent with fifty-six, while the equally populous Norfolk and Suffolk had only twenty-four and thirty-eight respectively. But the latter two counties were then dominated by a great nobleman, while in Kent at any rate the lesser gentry were warring among themselves for supremacy and naturally regarded a place on the Bench as a useful adjunct in the struggle. The lengths to which a man might go to regain a lost place are suggested by the following letter written in 1598: 'The means [by which] he came into [the commission of the peace] was by my Lord North. He made such a speech at my Lord North's [table] . . . that my Lord upon mere zeal procured him to be in the commission. And Sir Henry North for mere affection was content to take £200 off him and Mr Powell [chancery clerk] was more reasonable to take but bare £40 for restoring him to his former place.'[5]

The actual wording of the commission was newly formulated in 1590 by Sir Christopher Wray, the Chief Justice, and remained unchanged for the next three hundred years. Most significantly it preserved the essentially judicial nature of the office, authorizing the Justice to enforce the basic statutes for keeping the peace and inquiring by jury into stated offences. The new Justice then took the oath of office and the oaths of supremacy and allegiance, and unless his name was dropped from any future commission (which happened fairly often) he remained a magistrate for life, or until the death of the sovereign. Clearly the powers and responsibilities of the office made it important to make a careful choice of men; Cecil certainly took immense pains before the renewal of commissions to check the suitability of the names to be included. This remained a strong weapon in the government's disciplining of local worthies: if they misbehaved they were left off, despite their protests. But one doubts whether such thoughts would be uppermost in the minds of the great magnates as they sent in their recommendations. The guiding motive of Robert Devereux, Earl of Essex, was simply to build up his family territorial interests: in the 1580s, anxious to increase his influence in south-west Wales, he managed to get four of his men into the commission for Carmarthenshire and five for Cardiganshire.[6] In 1587 Burghley sought from the bishops a confidential report on the religious proclivities of the Justices in their dioceses, asking whether they were recusants or known to favour recusants.[7] But in its wisdom the Elizabethan government did not want to exclude from office any but the most uncompromising Roman Catholics, knowing doubtless that a man's allegiance might well be swayed by the attractions of public office. Thus they were content with at least an occasional show of outward conformity in the early years of the reign, and the Privy Council seems to have turned a blind eye when returns of the oath of supremacy were not being made into Chancery, that is to say, the oath due from the Justices by which they acknowledged the position of the sovereign as supreme governor of England in temporal and spiritual matters.

The actual number of active Justices within any one county is not always easy to estimate. Statutes imposed no limitation, except for the arbitrary settling of the Welsh counties at eight, probably because of their similarity in size.[8] Thus the commissions were flexible, and when, towards the end of the century, Lambarde noted the tendency for numbers to grow 'to the ouerflowing of each shire' this was a comment both upon the increasing prosperity of the gentry and the increasing popularity of the office. A list compiled in 1580 gives a total of 1,738 J.P.s for the whole country, ranging from Rutland with thirteen to Kent with eighty-three; Sussex with forty-seven and Suffolk with fifty-six were probably more typical. But these numbers could be misleading since it was the practice to include high officers of state, Judges of Assize and nobles with territorial interests, who were merely honorary and not acting Justices. Recent work on sixteenth-century Wiltshire illustrates this: in 1562 the commission showed thirty names, of whom five came from outside the county, the rest being made up of one earl, two barons and twenty-two country gentlemen.[9] Naturally the main body of the Bench was made up of country gentry, members of those long-established landed families whose names recur generation after generation as the local rulers of their shires: the Careys, Courtenays, Grenvilles, Raleighs, Tremaines and Fortescues in Devon; the Mildmays, Waldegraves, Harveys, Darrells and Capels in Essex; the Guises, Hicks, Masters, Berkeleys in Gloucestershire. It was natural that son should succeed father in office, and as each generation married and settled within the county so the network of family connexion grew, reflecting in miniature those family links within the Tudor House of Commons which Professor J. E. Neale has said are so numerous that they almost defy description.[10] In Cheshire Peter Warburton of Arley, himself a Justice for over fifty years, had four sons-in-law on the Bench, and Thomas Woodhay, on the commission for thirty years, was the father of one Cheshire Justice and father-in-law of three more. This was the sort of pattern that might be found in almost any other county at the time.

Although the majority of these men were landowners the Bench was by no means the preserve of gentle birth and it numbered among its members those who had concerns in industry and mining. In the west of England cloth-manufacturing districts some on the commission would be clothiers themselves or have close connexions with the business of cloth-making; the same was true in the north, particularly in the West Riding of Yorkshire. In the midlands there are several examples of families of Justices like the Strelleys and the Willoughbys in Nottinghamshire who had interests in mining, or of men on the Cheshire and Worcestershire Benches who owned salt-pans. But association with a craft carried with it a definite social stigma, and John Harington was rebuked by the Privy Council in 1582 for employing an apprentice in printing and engraving, 'that profession being a matter contrary to your quality and calling'. No such feeling attached to maritime ventures or to the seizure of prizes, activities which enriched Sir Carew Raleigh, Justice for Wiltshire and Dorset, nor did such lucrative occupations as trafficking in appointments or moneylending carry any loss of social prestige.[11]

The growing number of lawyers in Tudor society was reflected in the Bench and a legal competence was common among Justices. One sixth of the gentry on the Essex Bench between 1559 and 1596 were trained in the law, and one tenth of the Somerset Bench for the same period. In fact the general education which the Elizabethan and early Jacobean gentry received at grammar schools, universities and Inns of Court produced Justices who were undoubtedly better educated than in earlier centuries, possibly even more *thoroughly* educated than their eighteenth-century successors.[12] And for those whose formal education stopped short at the Inns of Court there were numbers of practical manuals produced, as the author of one put it, 'to further the good endevor of such gentlemen as bee not trained up in the continuall study of the Lawes'.[13] Marow's classic work on the subject had appeared in 1503, Fitzherbert's was published in 1538, and both remained in wide circulation until Lambarde's *Eirenarcha* of 1581 became the indispensable handbook for a century and more.

The wages of four shillings a day during sessions which had been instituted in the time of Richard II were still paid by the Sheriff from the fines and amercements but by this date they were generally expended on communal entertainment for the Bench. Otherwise 'the lawes do now and then cast them a trifle', as Lambarde put it, and a few statutes allowed fees for specific duties: 2s. 6d. for enrolling lands under 27 Hen. VIII c. 10; 12d. for taking an innkeeper's recognizance under 5–6 Ed. VI c. 25; 5s. a day, not exceeding three days, for attending sessions to enforce the Elizabethan labour code, and so on.[14] But in effect these men's services were unpaid and some private wealth was a prerequisite for those who wanted to become magistrates.

If the duties were virtually unpaid they were none the less onerous. They derived from two main sources. The commission of the peace gave to every individual Justice various powers to act as keeper of the peace in the county; it authorized two or more together to inquire into various offences and to hear and determine them; and collectively the whole Bench for any county was to sit as a publicly convened court in general sessions. This preserved the original judicial side of the office, its *raison d'être*, 'for the conservation of the peace'. But an even greater mass of duties devolved upon the magistracy from the succession of statutes which throughout the century was laying the whole responsibility for local administration firmly upon their shoulders. By the end of Elizabeth's reign Lambarde could list 309 statutes which in one way or another referred to the Justices, of which sixty had been made between 1485 and 1547, thirty-nine under Edward VI and Mary, and seventy-seven under Elizabeth – figures which show a steadily increasing momentum. Some Acts of course were merely repetitions, or had no more than temporary and local significance. But many more, above all the labour code and the Poor Law, opened up whole new fields of activity. Thus by the end of the sixteenth century the Justice might expect to find himself enforcing price regulations and recusancy laws; supervising the maintenance of bridges and highways; licensing alehouses and regulating wages; putting lads out to apprenticeship and giving relief to the poor and the aged, all as part of his routine duties.

Since the office of Justice was onerous and ill-paid, offering few apparent rewards but very many obvious burdens, how was it that a place on the Bench was so highly sought after in this period? In most counties there were more gentry than Justices and few held office for any length of time without interruption: they could always be removed from the commission in the sure knowledge that there were more aspirants to the Bench than there were places available. What was the attraction of office, an attraction so strong that in Norfolk, at any rate, men were prepared to spend years waiting and intriguing for office?[15] There are some obvious general human reasons: the wish to rule, the desire to serve the community. But more specifically, a clue is to be found in the factions and quarrels which abounded within the counties in the sixteenth and seventeenth centuries. If parliamentary elections, as Neale has shown, were the occasions for the rival groups to fight for seats, what more natural focus for the preliminaries to the battle than the Bench at Quarter Sessions? As early as 1565 Nicholas Bacon was complaining that many gentry wanted to be Justices for no better reason than 'to serve the private affection of themselves and their friends as in overthrowing an enemy or maintaining a friend, a servant, or tenant'. For a gentleman inclined to factiousness the office of Justice presented almost endless scope for harrying his local enemies. Bacon in fact went so far as to say that the Justices instigated more riots than they averted. Ironically enough Quarter Sessions itself offered an excellent opportunity for serious quarrels to break out since most Justices rode to sessions with their servants. The Russells and Berkeleys always brought five hundred armed supporters to the sessions at Worcester until Bishop Whitgift disarmed them and made the peace. In 1589 Sir James Croft appeared at the Hereford Assizes with from fifty to eighty armed followers to support his quarrel with the Coningsbys, and Sir William Holles of Haughton in Nottinghamshire would not dream of going to sessions at Retford without thirty proper fellows at his heels.[16] Instances such as these could be paralleled time and time again. It is therefore hardly surprising to find that a contemporary legal handbook contains a regular form of indictment 'For a Riotous Affray at the Quarter Sessions of the Peace'.

But as well as being the battleground for private quarrel and personal faction Quarter Sessions must also frequently have been the scene of dispute about matters of local administration. Of this however we know little for, as Hassell Smith points out, we are still very ignorant about what actually went on at Quarter Sessions.[17] But it is difficult to imagine most of the gentry of a county meeting to discuss a new rate or tax to deal with the sudden emergency of harvest failure, to arrange for the regulation of markets, to determine a tricky problem of Poor Law management, without finding themselves getting involved in controversial matters. Here, if only on a small scale, the questions of property and of individual rights would be hammered out by these magistrates practised in law, enunciating constitutional principles which those of them who were also Members of Parliament might later debate on the floor of the House of Commons. Who knows how many parliamentary speeches were first haltingly formulated among half a dozen neighbours in some local inn at an adjourned sessions to settle a rating problem or some kindred difficulty?

For often enough the Justices of the Peace, or at least the élite of the Bench, were also Members of Parliament, and if Westminster benefited from their knowledge and experience at the same time they could keep their fellow magistrates at home in touch with the mind of the central government. Men who had just passed bills in Parliament would be the best possible advocates of the importance of their efficient execution in the country; men who had themselves just been harangued personally by Elizabeth and inspired by her into a new diligence could infect the rest of the Bench with their loyalty to the throne in a way that the Judges reading their set pieces at the opening of Assizes could never do. With so many having a foot in both camps, the relations of central and local government were at once closer and more informal than has often been assumed. The haphazard survival of records has helped to perpetuate this misinterpretation. The Privy Council kept a note of its outgoing correspondence but not of the letters it received. Therefore a reading of the *Acts of the Privy Council* creates the impression of a mass of instruction sent down from London to the county Benches. But enough of the letters from the Benches to the Council have survived to make it clear that many of these harsh commands and rebukes were in fact occasioned in the first instance by the counties themselves, not infrequently by the members of one faction hoping to thwart the actions of their colleagues – and involve the Council in their machinations.

The main arena for faction, debate and the carrying out of the most important routine duties was Quarter Sessions, held four times a year and attended, in theory at least, by the entire Bench of magistrates. The time and place of sessions was generally decided by the Justices at their previous meeting for although they usually sat at the county town they did not always do so; particularly in the larger counties, they moved round a succession of lesser market towns. In theory all the Justices attended; in practice many clearly felt that their presence was only required at a meeting in the town nearest to them. As a result, in a county like Wiltshire where Quarter Sessions was held at a number of places attendance fluctuated greatly. The average in the later sixteenth century was from eight to eleven, but at Devizes in July 1576 there were only three Justices present and at the Michaelmas sessions in Chippenham in 1579 only two, while sixteen attended the Easter sessions at Warminster in 1586.[18] An examination of the Clerk of the Peace's lists shows that although some Justices attended only once a year many came to two or three Quarter Sessions, though on the same evidence in some years as many as half the members of any one Bench did not appear at Quarter Sessions at all.

Meeting in a room in the local castle, a cathedral chapter-house or an inn, Quarter Sessions gathered together not only the Justices but also the High Sheriff or his deputy, the coroner, the high and petty constables, the juries, the witnesses and the accused. Here, whatever its size, was a 'veritable court of law with all the organization and formality of a judicial gathering'.[19] The legal competence of the Bench was safeguarded in three main ways. In the first place a certain number of Justices on every Bench were ordered to be of the *quorum*, that is to say, they were to be men possessing legal training or else of considerable magisterial experience, which was in Lambarde's words 'so necessarie a light, without which all the labour is but groping in the darke, the end where of must needes be error, and dangerous falling'.[20] In addition each Bench had a *custos rotulorum*, an official specially chosen for sagacity and his social standing in the county. He was appointed by the Lord Chancellor, was always one of the *quorum*, and was held in deference by the other magistrates. He took custody of all writs, presentments and indictments, and was required to produce them at Quarter Sessions. Thirdly, the Clerk of the Peace, whose role really amounted to that of legal adviser to the Justices, was required by statute to be learned in the law, and his knowledge of correct procedure and legal precedent must often have saved the Justices from slips which would lay them open to censure by the higher courts. He was responsible for the correct framing of presentments and indictments, saw that the appropriate form of process was issued, that orders grounded on a statute were in accord with it, and generally that Quarter Sessions proceedings were kept within the bounds of the law.

Business at Quarter Sessions opened with the usual judicial formalities of empanelling juries and indicting the accused. The court had no power to hear civil suits and its jurisdiction did not extend to treason, forgery and some other major crimes, but this still left the Justices to deal with murder, assault, theft, witchcraft, poaching and the countless other crimes likely to be committed in the lawless countryside of the sixteenth century. Middlesex, where, admittedly, things were probably worse than in other parts of the country, shows case after case of manslaughter, assault, riot; men with iron-shod shares attacking and robbing servants; hasty quarrels in taverns ending in blows and death; even women fighting viciously, often in set contests.[21] The punishment which followed conviction was often no less brutal than the crime itself: flogging was common, hanging frequent, vagrants were branded, the parents of bastard children whipped. Some escaped their deserts because the Bench was unwilling to inflict such heavy penalties. Edward Hext, a Somerset Justice writing in 1596, believed that only a fifth of the crimes committed were actually brought to book.[22] Some criminals escaped justice however not through the leniency of the Bench, but for less praiseworthy reasons. Not infrequently the nobility, even the Justices themselves, took the side of the lawless and protected the wrongdoer. In Gloucestershire in the 1570s Lord Chandos used retainers armed with guns to protect his servants accused of highway robbery, while the Talbots and Cavendishes neatly saved a notorious poacher by putting their livery on his back.[23]

To draw a sharp distinction between criminal and civil matters at Quarter Sessions creates a false impression of sixteenth-century life and its problems. The Poor Law, which was of central importance to every Quarter Session and every Justice of the Peace, illustrates this well. Fear of poverty and unemployment was a major preoccupation of Tudor governments because the poor, who turned to rioting, crime and general lawlessness in times of famine and hardship, constituted a potential threat to security of life and property. It was as always this most urgent necessity of keeping the peace which drove sixteenth-century statesmen to put the Poor Law to the forefront of their domestic legislation. The devising of a Poor Law policy which survived in broad outline for nearly three centuries was one of the great achievements of the Tudors, and of the utmost importance in the development of local government.

Attempts to establish some system of poor relief were common to most countries of western Europe in the sixteenth century. But only in England did the Privy Council, towns and Justices together work out something which was to last until the beginning of modern times. They were faced in the early years with a complex problem, made worse by an increasing population and by sharp economic fluctuations, and one which was in fact much wider than the mere relief of poverty, since they were also concerned with providing rudimentary social services for the able-bodied who could not find work, children, vagrants and gypsies, the aged and impotent poor, the wandering and incorrigibly idle. From the passing of the important statute of 1531, which drew the distinction between the poor and the impotent who were allowed to solicit alms, and the able-bodied who were to be punished, the whole burden of administration was thrown upon the Justices. In 1536 another principle of vital significance appeared: the legal responsibility of each parish for the relief of its own poor. It would be tedious and unnecessary to recount all the various stages leading up to the famous Act of 1598 and its amplification in 1601.[24] These acts created the machinery for dealing with the problem of poverty by making each parish responsible for the poor within its boundaries: four householders were to be appointed annually at Easter by the Justices as overseers of the poor, and relief was to be financed by a poor rate levied upon all householders of the parish. The persons to be relieved were divided into three categories: children, able-bodied and infirm. Children were to be apprenticed; the able-bodied were to be set to work; the infirm and impotent were to be maintained in specially erected cottages. All this marks an extremely important stage in the process of state intervention for public welfare. In the first place it represents the recognition of the government's responsibility towards those unable to look after their own interests; secondly, it makes the Justice the central agent in putting this legislation into effect, and does not create any governmental and bureaucratic officials for the purpose; and thirdly, it uses the parish as a secular as well as an ecclesiastical unit.

The Poor Law legislation drew attention to, though it did not fully solve, one of the biggest problems and major weaknesses of

Tudor local government: finance. Most Quarter Sessions of the period have a dreary tale to tell of treasurers and constables unable to raise the money required of them. The Justices found themselves held responsible for the efficient working of what amounted to no more than a series of makeshift and uncoordinated devices. New officials, known as the Treasurers for the King's Bench and Marshalsea, appeared in 1592 as the result of a statute ordering maimed soldiers to be cared for from a local rate levied in their counties. Their powers were continuously enlarged after this to include the collection of funds for almshouses, houses of correction and hospitals. But since they, like the overseers and churchwardens responsible for the finances of the Poor Law, were appointed annually they remained more remarkable for their amateur status than for the competence which they brought to this wide range of activity.[25]

Regulation of wages and of labour, very much part of the problem of poverty, were dealt with by the Statute of Labour of 1563, which empowered the Justice to fix the rate of wages once a year, to bind apprentices to masters for seven years and to adjudicate in local labour disputes. These were intended as much for the health of the economy as for the welfare of the individuals concerned: the government recognized that if trade were to prosper the standard of manufacture must be maintained. But they also realized, and this was probably uppermost in their minds, that any falling off of England's exports, particularly textiles, would immediately result in industrial dislocation, unemployment and poverty, which in turn would constitute a threat to the peace and order of the countryside. Many other statutes concerning social and economic affairs had the same ends in view. Thus from 1552 it became one of the duties of the Justices to license alehouses and to keep a general oversight of the activities carried on within their walls, since it was only too easy for such places to become the refuge of rogues, vagrants and thieves. They were expected, as far as this was ever possible, to maintain reasonable prices for foodstuffs, particularly corn, and prevent speculation in times of shortage. From time to time they received orders from the Privy Council to search granaries, supply the markets and restrict export. In years of crisis, such as 1586–7, the Justices were actually appointing assistants to search the barns and find out how much each farmer had in store. 'We have visited the marketts, searched the barnes, storehouses and granyers of farmers and others and have in discretion appointed them a certeyne quantytie to be brought weeklie to the markett,' reported the Gloucestershire Justices in 1587. 'And we have sett downe several prices upon everie kind of graine . . . we will hereafter have care to see the same solde as may be beste for the relief of our poore neighbours.'[26] Such enthusiasm had in fact to be restrained by the Council which warned them not to defeat the purpose of the exercise by an unwise zeal, but to 'proceed with such good discretion as there shall grow no disorder or inconvenience thereby'.[27]

But in fulfilling other aspects of the government's economic policy, over-zealous enthusiasm was the last thing the Council had to guard against. It was of course never easy to ask the Justices to enforce laws which imposed irksome restrictions upon themselves and their neighbours, and when these touched upon their economic interests the Council faced a degree of unwillingness which often amounted almost to open rebellion. The Justices failed, for example, to enforce the statutes designed to control irregularities in the cloth industry. When in 1577 the government attempted to stamp out the unauthorized buying and selling of wool the Justices did the absolute minimum and were slow even in taking bonds from those dealers whose names had been given by the Council. While 'as touchinge the proclamacion made for restraynge of suche as had lycences to buye', they informed the Council several months later, 'we do not knowe sythence the makinge of the same that any persones here hath disobeyed yt.'[28] In despair the Council abandoned the attempt to obtain their cooperation and instead appointed ninety-one commissioners to have special oversight of the unlawful buying and engrossing of wool in twenty-one counties.[29] Statutes dealing with the processes of manufacture met with a similar fate. In this instance the Justices wanted freedom not restraint, and when their interpretation of what was best for the prosperity of the industry differed from that of the government they simply turned a deaf ear to commands, appeals and remonstrances.

The case with the statutes against enclosure was similar, possibly even more extreme, since more Justices were concerned with landholding and with the growing of wool than the manufacture of cloth. The government continued to attack the progress of enclosure by legislation and by commissions of inquiry throughout the Tudor period, concentrating on the social evils of depopulation and the conversion of arable land to pasture that were frequently connected with it. Yet the very fact that it was necessary to reiterate this, from the first general statute of Henry VII's reign (1489) against the pulling down of towns to the commission of 1607, shows the extent to which the government found themselves powerless to prevent it.[30] Enclosure as such was not the outstanding grievance of the rebels under Kett in Norfolk in 1549, but agrarian grievances in general bulked large in the programme of the rebellion. Immersed in their local feuding, for competition for wealth, place and prestige was as fierce here as anywhere, the forty-six local knights and gentry who at this time made up the county Bench had obviously little time or thought to spare for the economic problems of those beneath them. Their inactivity when faced with the rebellion, tantamount to abdication, is one of the most remarkable features of the whole episode. Nicholas Lestrange, lately Sheriff, actually fled by cock boat into Lincolnshire, taking Sir William Woodhouse with him and leaving his brother and son as hostages. The rest of the Justices seem to have gone to earth, lying low in their manor houses. Roger Woodhouse, who, by contrast, sought out the rebels with carts laden with bread and beer, was the one honourable exception. The Norfolk rebels turned to the central government as their main hope in enforcing its agrarian policy: their indictment lay against the local governors. 'It was the government on the spot which had to be supplanted, the man up at the Big House who needed a lesson.'[31]

Keeping open the internal communications of the country, for this was what the maintenance of roads and bridges amounted to, was another major preoccupation of the Justices. The Highways Act of 1555 ordered the annual election in every parish of surveyors whose duty it was to keep the roads in repair by exacting from every householder, cottager and labourer in the

41

parish either cart-service or manual labour. It is perhaps hardly surprising that only eight years later a further Act was passed empowering Quarter Sessions to inquire into and punish those surveyors guilty of neglecting their office. For among the many thankless tasks laid upon the shoulders of the individual Englishman in the sixteenth century this was peculiarly troublesome. The surveyors, serving without a salary, were expected to take their neighbours away from their fields and gardens to perform such unpalatable jobs as scouring out ditches and filling up potholes with loose dirt and stones. Complaints of the appalling road conditions were already loud in Tudor England and were to become louder still as the growth of wheeled traffic in the following century made them deteriorate even faster. Much Quarter Sessions time was given to fining a parish for failing to keep up a stretch of road within its bounds, and supervising the spending of the money thus collected more effectively.

In addition to these duties which were their major concerns in the field of administration – public welfare, social and economic regulations, the maintenance of communications – the Justices had also an infinite number of police duties which ranged from guarding their fellow countrymen from foreign invasion to dealing with those caught stealing partridges or swans' and hawks' eggs. If news came of the capture of English sailors by Barbary pirates the Justices of the maritime counties took up collections for their redemption. If a village or town suffered from fire the Justices quartered the homeless on the neighbouring parishes and appointed a committee to administer local voluntary relief. They could fine and imprison any person who spread abroad 'false, seditious and slanderous news' or who wrote, sang or spoke any 'phantastical or false prophecy'. The Reformation had brought further responsibilities. On the one hand the Justices were now expected to help hunt down recusants, on the other to guard the morals of their fellow subjects in such matters as over-fondness for costumes and sports above their station. Interference in the private lives of their neighbours was by no means confined to the Cromwellian regime and many an Elizabethan Justice took it upon himself to try and save a soul from falling into the errors of 'phanaticisme', or to lay a stern hand upon those pastimes which offended the Puritan conscience. Already in the 1590s some Somerset Justices were counselling together to get Church ales abolished and to have the alcoholic content of Somerset beer reduced, anxious to preserve the local youth from those junketings which might corrupt them and train them up in gaming, lascivious wantonness and sundry other disorders.[32]

The individual Justices had an important part to play in the campaign against recusancy. Probably the majority needed little prodding in their search for Popish priests. If Sir Francis Hastings, Justice for Leicestershire, is in any way typical the occasion of running one to earth was of great satisfaction. When William Hanse was brought before him he kept him prisoner in his house until the time of Assizes, 'and having examined him upon diverse poyntes I finde him so suttle, and settelled not to reveale anything' that he advised Mr Justice Meade that the Privy Council should be informed and accordingly sent them his full notes 'whereby his obstinacy will appeare, and must neede shew him greatly wedded to wil without reason'. The long letter to Walsingham reflects his burning zeal in the matter and the absolute conviction of the rightness of his actions.

Truly Sir I am perswaded that this viperous brode hathe spread it selfe farre in this nation. . . . I beseche the Almighty to direct your honor . . . to make you all the more careful if more may be that suche secrete seducers that stil run about to poyson the lande, & by privy whisperings to withdraw the simple sorte into a detestation of the presente government, & from thence by degrees of the governour her selfe, so you by your directions & commandements may disperse suche orders in every contry [county] to suche as are in authority under you as they may loke about them carefully. . . .[33]

Quite often the Justice, as in the case of Hastings, acted as an individual; other duties he performed in company with one or more fellow magistrates. It is interesting to note that of the total of 634 pages which make up Lambarde's four books, the second, which deals with the single magistrate, occupies 235. But the burden upon the individual Justice was being very considerably relieved by the growth of additional meetings which developed out of the work which two Justices were competent to do 'out of sessions', for which no jury was necessary. The use in a number of counties of the term 'Petty Sessions' by the end of the sixteenth century has led to much uncertainty and confusion.[34] It seems likely that the more informal three weekly sessional or monthly meetings and Petty Sessions were in fact identical in composition and function. Both were intended to secure the greater continuity of control over business which could be handled by any two Justices, and they also served as a useful occasion on which to collect from the high constables reports of matters due to come up at Quarter Sessions. In Essex, and this was probably as true elsewhere, they met originally to license alehouses. In one Norfolk division, as Sir Francis Walsingham described it in 1574, the local Justices would meet every three or four weeks to inspect the bridewell at Acle, and then, after dinner at an inn, settle disputes which used to be put to the old hundred court, and hear reports from the high constables of misdemeanours which came within the competence of Justices out of sessions.[35]

There were also coming into existence, though it is difficult to say with accuracy how widely, more formal sessions, designated 'special sessions', definitely constituted at a regular time and place, with a member of the *quorum* present, and a jury of presentment. Their most common purpose was to inquire into the execution of certain statutes. This was actually first ordered by the government in 1541–2 when they asked that a sessions with a jury be held at least six weeks before every Quarter Sessions, but was later repealed as being too great an imposition on the jury. Nevertheless the fact that they were common by Elizabeth's reign is comment enough upon the growing volume of local business, and it is interesting to see that the initiative comes in some instances from the central government, in others from the localities themselves – suggesting that these sessions were filling a real need. The central government seems to have been particularly glad to encourage the development of divisional sessions in times of emergency or of more intense activity, for they probably appreciated that this was a means not only of exploiting local knowledge to the full, but also of taking advantage of the services of all qualified Justices within the immediate area. Thus they ordered special sessions of inquiry during the years 1569–71, which saw an intensified campaign to suppress vagrants, in January 1587 when the Book of Orders regulating the grain supply was first issued, and again when it was reissued in the 1590s.[36] But in spite of the efforts of seventeenth-century governments, and particularly the activity of the Council, these sessions seem to have later lapsed, their failure being due, as in the original effort of 1563, to the difficulties of bringing together a jury in the interim periods between Quarter Sessions.

The basic unit in the hierarchy of local government was of course the parish, with its elected officers, constable, surveyors of the highroads and overseers of the poor. They, together with the high constables chosen for every hundred, constituted the rough and ready outdoor staff without whose help the Justices work would have been impossible. The use of the parish as a secular as distinct from a religious unit has commonly been hailed as yet one more example of the Tudor genius in reorganizing the machinery of local government. Yet while recognizing ing the truth of this one must beware of over-emphasizing the transition, for not only had the medieval parish its own elected officers and its own system of collecting and managing its revenues for communal purposes, but provision for the maintenance of the poor and the sick and for the upkeep of roads within the parish was already being made through the private benevolence of wealthier members, either by gifts in their lifetime or bequests in wills.[37] The new social legislation of the Tudors had much in common with medieval Christian piety, but its greatest departure was in making statutory what had hitherto been voluntary, and inevitably the succession of Tudor statutes made the very necessary tasks of the unpaid underlings both onerous and unpopular. The overseers and the surveyors have already been mentioned; the last of the triumvirate, the constable, was as much, in his own more limited territory, the maid-of-all-work as the Justice himself. Chosen for a year by ballot or otherwise, he was generally of the husbandman, artisan, small shopkeeper class, who found in his year of office that much of the execution of social and economic legislation fell to him in addition to his police duties, and that as well as chasing criminals he was also inflicting minor fines and punishment upon his own neighbours.[38]

The high constable was the intermediary between the petty constable and the Justices. In theory powers of appointment lay with the court leet of the hundred. In practice, by the sixteenth century if not earlier, these powers were passing either to Quarter Sessions or to the divisional Justices – a reflection of the new role of the high constable as essentially the servant of the Justice of the Peace. He was appointed for a length of time varying from three to ten years, a heavy fine being imposed upon anyone who refused to serve. In Wales he was required by statute (34–5 Hen. VIII c. 26 s. 70) to be a substantial yeoman or a gentleman, and this was general practice elsewhere since the performance of the office made considerable demands both upon time and money. He served for his hundred and within that area undertook military, police, financial and administrative duties. He was in effect the officer of the Justices, obliged to attend them at Quarter Sessions and special sessions and keep them informed of the state of the roads and alehouses, recusants and vagabonds – to present them in fact with a general report on the state of his locality, often based on information gleaned from the petty constables. He was responsible for collecting the various rates levied in the parishes, and paying them over once a quarter to the appropriate treasurers, a thankless task but one for which at least he was generally remunerated.[39] One of the most important functions was in connexion with wage regulation and labour movements. In the autumn after harvest the high constables ordered the petty constables to attend them at a 'statute sessions', to which they also summoned masters and servants, providing in fact what has been well called 'both a labour exchange and a registry of service contracts'.[40]

If a hierarchy of officials descended below the Justice there were also officials of high rank standing above him – he was in fact the pivot of the whole system. In any shire the High Sheriff held a position of rank and responsibility. Though the office was of medieval origin it was not until 1563 that each county had its own Sheriff,[41] for it had been customary for them to share. In his patent to the Sheriff the king declared '*commisimus tibi custodiam comitatus nostri*' ('we commit to you the keeping of our shire'), and in theory he was the governor of the county, collecting the royal dues, arranging for the election of knights of the shire, controlling the county gaol, and holding two courts, the tourn and the county court. In fact, in the Tudor period, and even more in the centuries which followed, his office deteriorated rapidly in status, until he found himself saddled with the pomp and ceremony of office together with the quite considerable financial outlay entailed, but little more.[42]

The Lord Lieutenancy had a different history, for it was the sixteenth century which saw the rise to power of this local military official, who in fact appropriated the military powers of the Sheriff. The office is only heard of in a few scattered instances in the earlier sixteenth century, commissions being issued, renewed and ended according to political exigencies, which were frequent enough: the north had given trouble long before the Pilgrimage of Grace in 1536 and continued to do so long afterwards; the 'west' (Dorset, Devon, Cornwall) was frequently seething with discontent, religious, political or economic, and quickly resorted to riots of protest; while in certain years, 1549 for example, the revolts spread through most counties of England. After the accession of Elizabeth these commissions were issued more and more systematically, in response to the internal unrest of the early years of her reign. The office gained its fullest importance during the war with Spain when the Privy Council turned constantly to the local nobility to organize the local levies, to see the men arrayed, trained and armed, prepared to defend the Crown against all foes. The Lord Lieutenancy was, as A. L. Rowse says, a typical Tudor creation, combining great panache with utility and responsibility.[43] But it illustrates well both the success and the limitations of the Tudor battle for peace and order. For even while the militia was being organized upon a territorial basis the tenants of the nobility, and even of the greater gentry, still recognized their quasi-feudal obligations to their lords. The relative importance of the two relationships was certainly shifting fast, but the duality was still not fully resolved by the end of the century; at the time of the Armada the national levies were supplemented by 1,500 foot and 1,600 horse supplied by the tenants and servants of the nobility and gentry. The Earl of Pembroke offered Elizabeth the use of a sizeable private army, and, though he warmly protested loyalty to the throne, the gesture has alarmingly medieval implications.[44]

In July and August 1595 Elizabeth ordered the Privy Council to look into the whole question of the Lord Lieutenancies. The investigation showed twenty-nine counties under seventeen Lord Lieutenants, all members of the nobility with the honourable and appropriate exception of Sir Walter Raleigh, Lord Lieutenant of Cornwall. Moreover nine of the seventeen, and those the most important, were members of the Privy Council.[45] It was inevitable that many of the most important like Burghley or Huntingdon could not be often resident in their counties, and so deputies were appointed in their place by direct commission from the Queen. The earliest mention of them comes in 1585, and their appointment probably reflects the more thorough organization of the later years of the reign. A judicial decision at the end of the century stipulated that there must be at least two deputy lieutenants per county. In fact there were usually more, particularly in the counties with exposed coastlines: the total came to two hundred for the fifty-two counties in England and Wales.

The office of deputy lieutenant in practice burdened the Justices with yet one more task, since the deputies were always chosen from the leading landowners in any county, which often meant from among the foremost Justices. They carried out instructions from the Lord Lieutenant or from the Privy Council, and their duties can well be seen in a set of orders issued by one Lord Lieutenant to his deputies in 1590. They were to muster the able men of the shire, select soldiers for the trained bands, list all armour and weapons, see to the supply of bullets and gunpowder, keep up the beacons, compel all gentlemen of good living to muster their bands – and see that their horsemen had cloaks of the same colour.[46] In addition they often found themselves saddled with financial duties, collecting loans imposed by the government, or in times of unrest with other necessary tasks such as regulating corn supplies and organizing markets. This must have added considerable strain to the already burdened Justice, for it was expected that the Lord Lieutenant should work closely with his neighbours: this was part of the common responsibility laid upon the county for law and order, the duty to determine how their county should be kept 'both in quiet from dangers of mutinies and rebellion, and also from offence of enemies'.[47]

Military affairs reflect clearly two of the main principles of Tudor local government: first, the government of the county itself was the responsibility of the landowners, nobility and gentry jointly; second, the Crown and the Privy Council gave its orders to the local rulers and expected to intervene if they were not duly executed. For the Privy Council did not allow the Justices to forget for long that they were under its supervision and control. As a succession of orders and letters laid new demands upon them, the Council did not hesitate to see that these were properly carried out nor was it slow in punishing cases of negligence. It was always willing to investigate complaints of neglect or oppression brought against Justices. Cases of maladministration might be heard in chancery or by the Justices of oyer and terminer, who were specially empowered to hear indictments on treasons, felonies and so on; after 1542 the Judges of Assize were empowered to hear charges of negligence or of abuse of power, and from 1543 King's Bench received a transcript of all processes before Quarter Sessions.[48] The rights of the individual, or at least of the articulate individual, were thus safeguarded to a certain extent against the amateur or the biased ways of the local magistrate. For the Justices themselves the Judges of Assize must have presented the most forcible reminder of this supervision. Twice a year, in Lent and again in June and July, Judges left Westminster to administer the law locally in the Assize courts. The Justices were required to meet them at the Assizes held for their respective counties: non-attendance was regarded as a sign of disrespect. Here the Justices found themselves sitting at the feet of the professionals, gaining instruction in difficult cases, receiving advice on interpretation of statutes or points of procedure.

The government found the Judges of Assize a most useful channel for bringing direct pressure to bear upon the local magistracy, and frequently at Assizes the Justices would learn what was uppermost in the mind of the Privy Council at the moment and how they were expected to respond. Any intensification of the campaign against poverty or recusancy, any tightening of military or economic regulation, would be introduced here.[49] It was not unusual for Elizabeth to call together those Justices and Judges of Assize who were in Westminster, sometimes at the beginning, sometimes at the end of the law term, and through the mouth of the Lord Chancellor to direct their attention to certain matters. In 1573 Sir Nicholas Bacon, who would normally have done this, was away and Burghley acted as Elizabeth's spokesman, delivering a splendid piece of oratory, to judge by what has survived.[50] Drawing attention to the dangers of the Puritans he elaborated his theme of the necessity for obedience and uniformity, likening England to a ship in a storm, and setting out the disasters likely to follow if the crew turned rebellious. The point was that the Queen had issued injunctions commanding uniformity in religion and that it was incumbent upon the Justices to see they were obeyed.

But what did all this amount to? Statutes, orders, exhortations, threats – if the counties were so disposed they were faithful and willing servants of the Crown; if they disagreed with the dictates of Westminster they resisted them or, equally effectively, neglected them. The early Tudor policy against enclosure and eviction touched the pride and the pockets of the landowners rather too closely, and practice fell far short of the fine parade of principles of social justice inscribed upon the statute book. The phrases concerning uniformity and supremacy sound magnificent, but in a predominantly Roman Catholic county such as Lancashire sympathetic magistrates sheltered their neighbours and allowed them to practise their Popish worship comparatively unmolested. In conception the Elizabethan Poor Law presents an impressive code of social welfare; in practice it was waived whenever local magistrates found its claims too demanding. On one thing at least Westminster and the shires agreed, and that was the promotion of law and order; though even here, as the succeeding century was to show, violence might be submerged rather than ended, and feud and faction died only a slow and lingering death.

References

1. L. Stone, *The Crisis of the Aristocracy 1558–1641*, Oxford University Press, 1965, p. 200.
2. The family head at this time of course governed not only the wife and children but also brothers, sisters, nephews, grandchildren, cousins and servants. The importance of the family in the social structure has been shown by Peter Laslett, *The World We Have Lost*, Methuen, 1965.
3. Stone, *op. cit.*, p. 208.
4. E. P. Cheyney, *A History of England from the Defeat of the Armada to the Death of Elizabeth*, Longmans, 1926, II, pp. 318–19.
5. A. Hassell Smith, review of B. Osborne, *Justices of the Peace 1361–1848*, 1960, in *The American Journal of Legal History*, 1961, v, pp. 285–6.
6. P. Williams, *The Council in the Marches of Wales under Elizabeth*, University of Wales, 1958, p. 119.
7. C. Read, *Lord Burghley and Queen Elizabeth*, Jonathan Cape, 1960, p. 421.
8. 34–5 Hen. VIII c. 26 s. 55. S. A. Peyton, *Minutes of Proceedings in Quarter Sessions held for the Parts of Kesteven in the County of Lincoln 1675–1695*, Lincoln Record Society, Lincoln, 1931, p. xxx.
9. In 1600 when the total had risen to fifty-two the proportions remained about the same, with 6 honorary members, 7 members of the local nobility and 37 country gentry, together with the Bishop of Salisbury and his chancellor. J. Hurstfield, 'County Government 1530–1660', *Victoria County History of Wiltshire*, University of London, Institute of Historical Research, 1957, v, p. 89. (After this referred to as *V.C.H.*)
10. *The Elizabethan House of Commons*, Jonathan Cape, 1941, pp. 312–13.
11. M. G. Davies, *The Enforcement of English Apprenticeship 1563–1642*, Cambridge, Massachusetts, 1956, p. 178.
12. See K. Charlton, *Education in Renaissance England*, Routledge, 1965; J. Simon, *Education and Society in Tudor England*, Cambridge University Press, 1966.
13. Cheyney, *op. cit.*, p. 316.
14. Peyton, *op. cit.*, p. xxxi.
15. This paragraph owes much to the extremely interesting and provocative review by A. Hassell Smith mentioned above (note 5).
16. Stone, *op. cit.*, p. 231.
17. *op. cit.*, p. 283.
18. Hurstfield, *op. cit.*, pp. 91–2.
19. Cheyney, *op. cit.*, p. 327.
20. Peyton, *op. cit.*, p. xxx.
21. Cheyney, *op. cit.*, pp. 331–2.
22. See E. M. Leonard, *The Early History of English Poor Relief*, Cambridge University Press, 1900, p. 126.
23. Stone, *op. cit.*, p. 230.

24. For a brief account, see J. R. Tanner, *Tudor Constitutional Documents*, Cambridge University Press, 1940, pp. 469 ff. E. M. Leonard's book (cited above) remains the standard work, though it needs revision in some respects, together with S. and B. Webb, *English Poor Law History*, I, *The Old Poor Law*, Longmans, 1927.

25. For a good account of county finances in the Tudor period, see Hurstfield, *op. cit.*, pp. 97–8.

26. Quoted B. Osborne, *Justices of the Peace*, Sedgehill Press, Shaftesbury, 1960, p. 45.

27. *Acts of the Privy Council 1586–7*, pp. 59–60, quoted C. A. Beard, *The Office of Justice of the Peace in England*, New York, 1904, p. 132.

28. P. J. Bowden, *The Wool Trade in Tudor and Stuart England*, Macmillan 1962, p. 136.

29. No information about them appears to have survived so we cannot judge how effective they proved. See Bowden, *op. cit.*, p. 140.

30. For an analysis of the way in which the statutes change over the period and reflect a growing understanding of local differences and changing economic conditions see Maurice Beresford, 'Habitation versus Improvement: The Debate on Enclosure by Agreement,' in *Essays in the Economic and Social History of Tudor and Stuart England*, ed. F. J. Fisher, Cambridge University Press, 1961, pp. 40–70.

31. S. T. Bindoff, *Ket's Rebellion*, Historical Association, 1949, pp. 18–19.

32. M. C. Cross, 'An example of lay intervention in the Elizabethan church', *Studies in Church History*, ed. G. J. Cuming, Nelson, 1965, II, p. 280.

33. Sir Francis Hastings to Sir Francis Walsingham, 8 April 1582, Huntingdon Library H. A 5086, H. M. C. Hastings, II, p. 36. I owe this reference to Dr Claire Cross.

34. The Webbs are here particularly misleading in saying that these early Petty Sessions were identical with divisional special sessions; see their *English Local Government: The Parish and the County*, Longmans, 1906, pp. 40 ff.

35. Davies, *op. cit.*, p. 213.

36. Leonard, *op. cit.*, pp. 80–81, 84.

37. See W. K. Jordan, *Philanthropy in England 1480–1660*, Allen & Unwin, 1959.

38. See further Cheyney, *op. cit.*, pp. 403–8.

39. For a clear and vivid account of his duties, see Peyton, *op. cit.*, pp. xlii–xlv.

40. See Davies, *op. cit.*, pp. 190 ff.

41. Peyton, *op. cit.*, p. xv, note 2.

42. See the following chapter for a fuller discussion of the Sheriff in connexion with ship-money, which brought him into the limelight for the last time, in unique and unfortunate circumstances.

43. *The England of Elizabeth*, Macmillan, 1950, p. 383.

44. Stone, *op. cit.*, p. 206.

45. G. Scott Thomson, *Lords Lieutenants in the Sixteenth Century*, Longmans, 1923, Appendix B.
46. Cheyney, *op. cit.*, p. 367.
47. Scott Thomson, *op. cit.*, p. 78.
48. W. S. Holdsworth, *History of English Law*, Methuen, 1923, IV, pp. 78 ff., 162 ff.
49. J. Lister, *West Riding Sessions Rolls*, Yorkshire Archaeological and Topographical Association, Record Series, 1888, II, pp. 397–9; Cheyney, *op. cit.*, pp. 381–5.
50. Read, *op. cit.*, p. 117.

CHAPTER THREE

1603–1660
Faction and Feud

EARLY in 1642 the discontents of England erupted into open violence. By the autumn of that year organized military operations had begun; by the end of the war homes had been looted, farms burned, churches and cathedrals desecrated, and some one hundred thousand Englishmen had died.[1] Why and how did the Great Rebellion come about? How was it that men could take up swords against brothers, cousins, neighbours? In spite of continuing academic discussion we still do not fully know the answers to these questions. The historians disagree. Some still pay lingering attention to the hypothesis that would make it a class war, the final struggle in which bourgeois England triumphed over feudal England. Others are in agreement with James Harrington who as long ago as 1656 propounded the idea of the fundamentally economic nature of the war. Others again would insist that only the fervour of religion could have driven men to such extremes and that the English civil war should take its place among the religious wars of seventeenth-century Europe. One thing however is becoming increasingly clear, that the perspective is distorted if attention is focused mainly upon London and upon politics at the national level. The localities hold the key to any true understanding of events, for local loyalties and local feuds were of the very stuff of life to the seventeenth-century nobility and gentry. Parliament might be the ultimate arena for constitutional debate, but it would be a mistake to take Parliament as a mirror of the nation. In any case, and this was most particularly true of the early years of the seventeenth century, it was still only an occasional and irregular part of government. From November 1640 onwards it was sitting almost continuously, but between 1603 and 1629 it sat for only a total of four and a half years, and between 1629 and the spring of 1640 it did not meet at all. The mainspring of government was the Privy Council with its executive, the Justices of the Peace. The country gentry were the political nation.

The county in the seventeenth century was much more than a geographical or administrative unit. It was, in a sense, a community; a society with its own government, its recognized leaders, its internal rivalries, and a society which could on occasion speak with one voice. Provincial patriotism was a power whose strength it is sometimes difficult for twentieth-century minds to grasp. But unless this is remembered, as Tawney has said, 'both the social life and the politics of the age must remain closed books'.[2] Pride in their native counties spurred that great outburst of topographical writing which produced a succession of county histories between roughly 1560 and 1660. 'Lest my native countrie [county] should any longer lye obscured with darkness,' wrote William Burton of Leicestershire in 1622, 'I have adventured (in some sorte) to restore her to her worth and dignitie.' When William Lambarde, whose *Eirenarcha* was to make him the mentor of the Justices, published his *Perambulation of Kent* in 1576, he dedicated it to his fellow countrymen: 'I know not (in respect of the place) unto whom I may more fitly send it than unto you, that are either bred or well brought up here, or by the goodness of God and your owne good provision are well settled here; and here lawfully possess, and are neere unto sundry of those things that this book specially speaketh of.' This was most fitting: the county gentry formed the backbone of county society as they did of county government. Difficulties of travel and the rapidly worsening state of the roads encouraged local landowners to stay at home and play their full part in local affairs. Only for a few was London a magnet strong enough to draw them from the management of their estates and the company of their fellow landowners.[3] Speaking the local dialect, their ambitions probably went no further than the wish to see their sons established upon the ancestral acres and their daughters safely married to the sons of some neighbouring estate. Within many counties intermarriage was very frequent indeed. At the time Mary Honywood died in the 1630s, for example, her 367 descendants brought nearly all the gentry of Kent on to a single genealogical tree.[4] At Quarter Sessions, the natural meeting place for the gentry, a man might hope to sit beside his sons and sons-in-law, brothers and cousins. Between 1625 and 1640 as many as thirty-five Somerset Justices were linked by marriage alliances contracted during the previous generation or two.

The seventeenth-century counties might have many common features, tightly knit family relationships being one of them, but the actual structure of local society shows a wide range of variations. A recent historian has gone so far as to say that 'in some respects the England of 1640 can be likened to a union of partially independent shire-states, each with its own distinct ethos and loyalty.'[5] A landowner's loyalties and aspirations would naturally be influenced by the shape of the society in which he found himself, whether it was one dominated by a single family or an all-powerful peer; one in which there was a coterie of twenty or thirty leading gentry; or one where two great houses contested the leadership and split the county between them.

In Kent no one family was dominant. Instead there was a group of twenty to thirty leading families of comparable standing, mostly indigenous to the county and deeply rooted in its soil. Those descended from mercantile wealth were confined to a small area near London, while the great majority were derived from the minor gentry of the thirteenth to fifteenth centuries: the Derings, Twysdens, Boyses, Finches, Honywoods and Knatchbulls, men who had risen to positions of authority in their local society by careful estate management and by prudent marriage with Kentish heiresses.[6] More commonly a county was dominated by one family, Essex by the Barringtons, Lancashire by the Derbys. Suffolk shows an interesting variant on this. Here was an oligarchy of county families, but one that recognized the unquestioned leadership of the Barnardistons, whose unofficial suzerainty owed as much to their moral stature as Puritans as to their riches and antiquity. By the mid seventeenth century they were headed by Sir Nathaniel, upon whom, when a Member of Parliament was to be chosen, 'the thoughts, eyes and resolutions of all men were fixed, and all cried for a Barnardiston, a Barnardiston'.[7]

The personal and family feuds in Leicestershire were so notorious by this time that a contemporary pamphlet, *Terrible News of Leicester*, said the county was 'like a cockpit, one spurring against another'. In the time of Elizabeth the third Earl of Huntingdon had run the county like a private bailiwick.[8] But in the following century the family's domination was far less secure, and a restless gentry were making their protests, some as audibly as Sir Henry Shirley and Sir Anthony Faunt who in 1628 were severely punished by the government for the aspersions they cast upon the character of the fifth Earl. Opposition was led by the Greys under Henry Earl of Stamford, and Clarendon believed the county was split between the families with the allegiance of the county gentry divided between them. The Greys drew their supporters chiefly from the south and east of the county, and claimed a majority of the great county families: the Caves, Babingtons and Ashbys who had done well out of monastic lands, the Herricks and Dicies, merchants turned landowners. To the Hastingses rallied the Shirleys, Turvilles, Skeffingtons, Poulteneys and Beaumonts, together with many small squires of less distinguished lineage. The personal jealousies and animosities of these two camps were to be of the greatest importance in the political crisis leading to the Civil War.[9]

Divisions were equally acute in Somerset. Until the creation of the Earl of Marlborough and Baron Poulett in the 1620s Somerset had no nobility, but its social hierarchy was made up of twenty-five families, generally though not invariably headed by a knight. The most significant of these was Sir Robert Phelips who for nearly a quarter of a century, until his death in April 1638, contested the supremacy of the county with Lord Poulett. Until 1614 they had been good if not intimate friends; but when in that year Poulett carried both county seats Phelips never forgave him, and from then on hardly a year passed without one or the other attempting to discredit his enemy. Phelips was the greatest man on the Bench; Poulett was the more powerful in the militia. In the absence of Parliament they made county government the scene of their battles, and only a very exceptional Justice, such as John Harrington, was capable of standing aside; most joined one side or the other. 'Friendship, ambition, family ties, animosity, ignorance and weakness all played their part in enticing the majority of local governors into one camp or the other. Sometimes the allegiance was transitory. More often it was firm, and such was the rancour of the struggle, few men were inclined to cross over.'[10]

The county was indeed a compact society, but one which held potentially explosive material: the local factions which tore local society apart were not far below the surface, and likely to erupt if the spark was ignited. It would be a mistake to assume from the emphasis on inter-marriage and family connexion that this naturally bred a harmonious society. 'Neighbourhood, kinship and at times, the semi-dynastic influence wielded by a local magnate are more potent than most other grounds of union or division.'[11] Nobility and gentry divided only too easily into quarrel and feud. The social categories invented by historians are, as Charles Wilson has reminded us,[12] not only unhelpful but misleading in suggesting more or less solid classes distinguishable from each other. The reality was faction: court faction, country faction, the ins and the outs, the haves and the have-nots.

The Tudors had won their battle against the cruder forms of violence: so much is apparent from the preceding chapter. The keeping of retainers, the fortifying of castles and the accumulation of arms was now a thing of the past. But, such is human nature, men still fought over issues of property and status. 'What might ostensibly appear as a quarrel over a piece of land or an office, in fact was at bottom a struggle for position and authority within the county society.'[13] 'What was sought was the recognition of the other local governors and the mass of the county's populace below them that the triumphant magnate was the magnate of magnates.'[14] The nobility fought to acquire or to retain pre-eminence in the distribution of county patronage; the gentry strove for entry to the Bench or for appointments to local commissions. The history of Somerset has shown us how a feud between two leading county families could carry with it an entire county. And moreover, since the protagonists sought the support of the Justices and the deputy lieutenants, they brought their divisions into the courtroom and the county array. As the threat of war grew closer the existence of such faction, potential or actual, was to become increasingly serious for King Charles, for two reasons. In the first place, society was already so fragmented that division and alignment on opposing sides came easily, almost naturally. And secondly, it impaired most seriously the smooth running of the local machinery just at a time when Charles needed, more than ever before, to organize his support in the shires and to be able to rely upon the swift and efficient execution of his orders. As the history of ship-money and the militia was to show, in county after county, the king's most urgent need for men and money was to be frustrated by the lesser struggles of local men.

The routine concerns of local government in the seventeenth century were not, at least in the early years of the century, markedly different from those which faced the Elizabethan Justice of the Peace. The main lines of local administration had been promulgated and they continued to be put into force: economic regulation, the care of roads, recusancy, the labour code, the Poor Law, and, above all, the maintenance of order and the punishment of minor criminals. As in the sixteenth century the most alarming problem which faced central and local government was that of 'the poor', the collective title by which the lower orders of society were known. These, if Gregory King's estimates in 1696 may be taken as any guide, formed 3·3 million out of a population of 5·5 million. They were the unprivileged, the common, the anonymous; they ranged from small shopkeepers, tradesmen and artisans through mechanics, labourers and cottagers to paupers, vagrants, thieves and beggars.[15] They were not all destitute, nor destitute all the time, but a large proportion were potentially destitute and over them hung the threat of poverty, unemployment and starvation, either when times were bad or as they grew old and could no longer support themselves. To keep alive they must either turn to crime, depend upon charity – or receive the support of the state.

Poor relief in the seventeenth century was of course based upon the great Elizabethan Poor Law code, and its success or failure reflected very much the fluctuating vigour of the Privy Council in urging its efficient administration in the localities. In the last year of the reign of Elizabeth the Duke of Stettin, admittedly always given to eulogies about England, had painted a glowing picture of the Poor Law at work: 'For in all England they do not suffer any beggars except they be few in number and outside the gates. Every parish cares for its poor, strangers are brought to the hospital . . . those that have come from distant places are sent from one parish to the other, their wants being cared for until at last they reach their home.'[16] Yet only a few years later Coke was complaining that 'rogues soon swarmed again', and the author of a tract of 1606, a converted highwayman anxious for the reformation of his fellow sinners, stated that 'Beggerie and Theeverie did never more abound.'[17] Allowing for exaggeration on both sides it is nevertheless clear from such contemporary comment and from more official sources that the Justices were growing careless and in many places scarcely executed the law. In fact Miss Leonard came to the conclusion that there was during these years a very real likelihood that the Poor Law would become obsolete.

As always, it was a time of crisis and scarcity which spurred the Privy Council into activity. Harvest failure and a crisis in the cloth trade in 1622–3 threatened serious social dislocation. The government was anxious to provide work and to lower the high price of bread since, particularly in the cloth-making counties, workmen were being turned off by their employers. In February 1622 a letter was sent to the Justices in ten counties which manufactured cloth 'to call before you such clothiers as you shall thinke fitting and to deale effectually with them for the imployment of such weavers, spinners and other persons as are now out of worke'.[18] But as the crisis continued the impossibility of such a policy became clear. The Judges of Assize reported that they had interviewed the clothiers of Gloucestershire and had persuaded them to keep their men on for a fortnight: they were unable to do more. Early in 1623 matters were no better and a series of relief measures were undertaken for selling corn under cost to the poor and finding work for the unemployed. The good harvest of that year brought some improvement and the Privy Council's temporary spurt of activity was allowed to die away again, for between times of emergency the government's interest seems to have lapsed completely. But again the years

1629 and 1630 brought the all too familiar story of harvest failure, of corn shortage and unrest, though there was now also the threat of plague to add to the general fears. In this case however the emergency was to produce measures of lasting significance.

The publication of the Book of Orders reflected Charles I's determination to re-invigorate the Poor Law machinery. But in fact it did much more than this. For when on 5 January 1630/1 a commission under the Great Seal nominated almost the whole Privy Council as commissioners for the poor it also enabled them to inquire into the working of 'other public services for God, the king, and the commonwealth'. If the execution of the Poor Law was to be revitalized the way was clearly also open for inquiry and reform in other spheres of local government. This in fact marked the beginning of an attempt, unparalleled in the history of the magistracy, to instil a new vigour into local administration. The Book of Orders has been called 'the most concerted effort, almost until our own times, to make the statute book an effective reality'.[19] It contained little or nothing that was new: that was not its purpose. But it set forth clearly and succinctly the law as it stood, so that even the most unlearned Justice might know what the central government expected of him. All the orders had in fact appeared during the past thirty years: but now they were presented as a unity, one whole programme of Poor Law, peace, watch and ward, maintenance of tillage, apprenticeship, regulation of alehouses, demanding intensive execution. There was nothing new either about the methods: the Privy Council relied on the Judges of Assize in circuit and the already existing machinery of monthly meetings were extended and in some cases regularized.

The government also made use of that modern device, the report. At these monthly meetings reports were made from the parishes of measures taken and at their six-monthly Assizes the Judges received reports from the Justices. This amounted in fact to a series of inquisitions: the commissioners charged the Judges of Assize and then inquired of them on their return; the Judges charged and questioned the Justices at Assizes, and the Justices in their turn interrogated the subordinate officers at Petty Sessions.

By this means the Council's own intensity was transmitted downwards – and in these early years it had about it a note of moral fervour: the good laws of the kingdom had not been executed 'especially from the neglect of dutie in some of Our Justices and other Officers, Magistrates, and Ministers of the Peace'.[20] How long this early intensity lasted is less certain. In April 1632 a sharp letter went out to every Sheriff: 'whilest ye businesse was fresh it was well putt in execucion, and much good came of it; but now of late [there] is so much slacknesse as all retournes againe to ye former course.' The Sheriff was to remind the Justices of their duties as set out in the Book, to commend those who had done well and so to encourage them, and to make sure that the Judges received a report of their performance. By 1635 however the Council's own energies and interests were turning elsewhere, to the business of ship-money. But in their place the Judges of Assize continued to bring pressure to bear upon the Justices, and it became their responsibility, which they pursued energetically, to see that the Book of Orders was not forgotten and that the programme that it had instigated was not allowed to fall by the wayside.

The early years of the programme still reflected its initial impulse: until 1634 when the severe scarcity of corn was abated Poor Law enforcement was emphasized, together with the measures familiar in times of emergency: the control of markets, the preservation of the grain supply and so on. Wealthier parishes were ordered to contribute to the poor rates of those parishes with so many paupers that they could not support them unaided, and the augmented funds were to be used for the impotent poor and to purchase stocks of materials to set the able-bodied to work. Sturdy vagabonds were dealt with more fiercely than they had been since the days of Elizabeth; the Irish ones were sent home, the native to the houses of correction. The apprentice laws were enforced with a vigour that had long been unfamiliar. Widespread unemployment together with the food shortage of 1629–30 meant that there was a greater number of children than usual either to be apprenticed or to be supported out of the parish funds. Generally there had been enough artificers able and glad to have an apprentice; now the economic dislocations meant that far fewer were willing to take them, and the Justices had to resort to forcible apprenticing, a move which often proved extremely unpopular. Thomas Coningsby, a Herefordshire Justice who was rash enough to state in Petty Sessions that enforced apprenticeship was illegal, and who repeated it when challenged before the Privy Council, was discharged from the commission and fined £100 in Star Chamber.[21] Few took their suit as far as this: when threatened with Assizes they generally climbed down, probably because they knew that if they sufficiently maltreated the apprentice assigned to them they would be rid of him soon enough, either through his absconding or by his being released from his indentures through danger of being flogged or starved to death. Unlicensed purveyors of drink also felt the attention of the magistracy upon them, and if a sum of the amount of £7 13s. 5d. could be raised from the 3s. fines imposed upon unlawful alehousekeepers and drunkards at the Bridgwater Petty Sessions in 1631 it suggests that many who had for years been quietly brewing ale for their neighbours were at last being brought to account.

After 1634, with a certain slackening of pace in the Poor Law implementation, emphasis shifted almost imperceptibly to the punishment of vagrants and other offenders at Petty Sessions. A Privy Council order of January 1633/4 extended the power of Justices and constables to apprehend vagrants in flight from other counties. The making of false passes by professional beggars who tried to pose as returned soldiers was effectively repressed, and the numbers of crimes committed by vagabonds showed a marked decline. In fact vagrancy, admittedly one of the minor social evils but a potential source of crime and a threat to security, was subdued during this time far better than it had been for the previous forty years. 'Nowe wee haue fewe or noe wanderers' – the boast comes from the Justices of the High Peak of Derbyshire in 1635, but throughout the 1630s similar claims were made from almost every corner of the country. One district of Leicestershire painted a rosy picture of their contented pauper population, in which the poor were set to work and the young taught knitting, so 'that yong people and children may receive imployment and fitting educacon and soe avoide idlenes and lewdenes of life'.[22] A thoroughly detailed report made in March 1636/7 (when some slackening of the original effort might have been expected) relating to the sixty parishes of Bassetlaw hundred in Nottinghamshire showed that in forty-five of them provision had been made for employing the poor.[23] From Buckingham came details of a most thoroughgoing organization: five hundred people were examined, their ages and occupations noted, and work was provided for those needing it. The poor 'of good disposicon', added a final note, not without a touch of complacency, 'are glad they are thus settled without begging and settle themselves seriouslie to their labour'. Some of the reports sent in to the Council from the more backward or outlying districts seem to suggest that the activity they so proudly record is in fact something new. Thus when the Justices of certain divisions of Radnorshire say that they have appointed overseers and organized the provision of stocks it seems to suggest that little in this line had been done before. A series of documents from Westmorland and several reports from Lancashire dating from 1638 indicate that a compulsory system of poor relief had only lately been established in the northern counties.[24] That the tentacles of the central government had at last reached such outlying districts must be counted not least among the successes of conciliar activity in this decade.

Apprentices, vagrants, maltsters and brewers, impotent poor and able-bodied poor, alehousekeepers and petty thieves, all felt the force of the Justices' hand upon them during these ten years as they had not felt it for many years before. Such widespread activity created its own momentum, and the withdrawal of the Privy Council seems to have disturbed the pattern remarkably little. It seems doubtful how much of local government, and above all of the administration of poor relief, would have survived the dislocation and confusion of the Civil War without the achievement of the Book of Orders. For nine years Justices and overseers had been drilled, parishioners had been compelled to pay rates, and the general population had become accustomed to the organization of poor relief.

The means used by the Book of Orders were almost as important as the ends which it achieved. Much of the burden fell upon the Justices out of sessions, and upon the lesser officials of the hundred and the parish, and as a direct result of this Petty Sessions established for itself an indispensable role in local government. It was held regularly and at a recognized place; the Justices of the division and their subordinates would be present; it became in fact a court on which Quarter Sessions relied for nearly all its out-of-sessions work. Barnes claims that local government saw no institutional development in the five centuries between the establishment of Quarter Sessions and the creation of County Councils so important as the advent of Petty Sessions. 'Petty sessions could not be eclipsed by the county council, and it may yet outlive Quarter sessions.'[25] Primarily throughout the 1630s the meeting at which Justices and lesser officials met to put into execution the Poor Law, it in fact proved so convenient for much other local business that it became a permanent part of the structure of local government.[26]

From 1634-5 the main interests of the Privy Council were diverted from the promotion of the Book of Orders to the collection of ship-money, an undertaking which reflects rather less credit on Charles I and his years of personal government. The writ for ship-money issued in October 1634 to maritime ports and counties was nothing unusual, and the needs of promoting the war and of protecting the fishing fleet from privateers made it seem a reasonable demand. Only with the issue of the second writ in the following year did it become apparent that, in his desperate search for money, Charles was intending to make this both a permanent and a general levy. The writ was sent to the High Sheriff, who was made directly and personally responsible to the Council for its collection and who thus, for the last time in his history, found himself thrust to the fore of local government. Nor did the Council let him forget this. From January 1636/7 onwards they demanded fortnightly reports of the progress of his collection: Mr Edward Nicholas, clerk to the Council, keeping his book of correspondence, brought every Sheriff under his unrelenting scrutiny. What made the hapless Sheriff's task even more bitter was that he did not gain his freedom at the end of his year in office: he was still personally accountable for the arrears which remained unpaid. In 1640 in Somerset there were still four ex-Sheriffs trying hopelessly to collect ship-money for their respective years.[27]

The Sheriff was to work through the high constables, who in their turn were to collect the money from the subordinate officials within their hundred. The method of rating was theoretically the existing county rating, but, and here the Privy Council introduced what was to prove a disastrous alternative, the Sheriff might take into account personal as well as real property when rating the more prosperous members of the community. Here was a contradiction: the Sheriff was to convoke meetings of raters, 'substantial men' from every parish and tithing within the hundred, yet at the same time he was empowered to set aside this rate and submit his own. The opposition was quick to seize and to exploit these anomalies in the divergence between the assessment from 'common payments' and the Sheriff's own assessment. And opposition there was, from every level of society, landowners, merchants, yeomen, freeholders, towns and parishes corporately. Some protests reached Whitehall, others got no farther than the county town. Such a situation presented an admirable arena for the play of local faction, and in Somerset Sir Robert Phelips and Lord Poulett clashed once again. When in 1636 Sheriff Bassett disallowed the rate made by Phelips and the raters of the hundred of Tintinhill, Stawell, a landowner in the hundred and Poulett's closest ally, told the Council that this was due to Phelips's determination to stir up trouble. Phelips replied that Stawell had insidiously prevailed upon the Sheriff to impose the new rate. Charles personally heard the pair of them out before the Privy Council, and sent them home admonishing them to lay aside their differences and join together in the service of their King and country.[28] But it cannot have been easy to convince men that the payment of such a tax was a necessary act of loyalty to the throne, and if this was difficult in 1636 it became no easier in the succeeding years. In fact, as the King's financial stringency grew so did the opposition. Hampden's case in 1637 gave them a martyr, and gentry, yeomen and husbandmen attacked ship-money in the most effective way possible: they simply refused to pay.

When in June 1640 the High Sheriff of Lincolnshire wrote to Edward Nicholas a candid report upon the impossibility of collecting ship-money he received only the angry response 'that his excuses are frivolous and he is to execute writt or shall answere for his owne neglect'.[29] Where is one to apportion the blame for this more or less total failure? Does it represent extensive corruption and perversion by the local officials? Does it show that the shires could when necessary become the voice of active political opposition? Much of the responsibility lay with the Privy Council. Its plans were not only unrealistic but ill constructed. It laid this heavy burden upon the shoulders of the High Sheriff alone, yet when, because of the rating disputes, his authority was challenged locally, it did not always support him. If the counties had been re-rated for the tax by the whole Bench of Justices this might have done something to quell the opposition within the ranks of the gentry, and the lower orders would have been faced by an authority familiar to them. As it was the Sheriff stood alone, driven by the Council and harassed in the shires. The high constables, however well intentioned in the first place, soon found themselves torn between irreconcilable loyalties, loyalty to the Sheriff as superior and loyalty to their peers, the yeomen and minor gentry who, at each dispute, grew bolder in challenging the tax and withholding payment. That ship-money was collected at all successfully in the early years was due in large measure to the grooming these lesser officials had received from the Book of Orders. But both the theory and the practice presumed too far and, in the conflict of loyalties produced among those levying the tax and those paying it, it was loyalty to the King which suffered most.

The failure of the ship-money levy was matched by the failure, in those vital years 1638–40, of the militia. When Charles turned north in November 1638 to subdue his rebellious subjects he found himself faced with an ignominious situation where the men of the county militias were not prepared to turn out to defend his interests. The roots of this failure went back to the early years of his personal rule when the deputy lieutenants should have been bringing the local militia up to its full force of competence. For with the virtual withdrawal of the Lord Lieutenant from active concern the main responsibility devolved upon the dozen or so deputies (often under the *de facto* leadership of a 'chief deputy' chosen from among themselves) who were squires and land-owners, the majority of them also Justices, having no other qualification than that it was naturally assumed that they were the leaders of their local society. The weaknesses of this haphazard system were exposed when local faction contended for the supremacy of the militia, as in Somerset where the battle of Poulett and Phelips undermined the authority of the deputy lieutenants and disrupted the military organization of the county.[30]

The militia of the early seventeenth century was, at least on paper, reasonably organized and armed. But as the years went on the machinery was allowed to grow rusty and the deputy lieutenants lax, until the morale had disappeared from the whole set-up. There was little provision for the maintenance or renewal of the original weapons, so that, unless confiscation from a local Papist should add a coat of mail or a pistol to the collection, arms and armour probably had a distinctly antiquarian flavour. Competent officers were not easy to find: the deputy lieutenants themselves would take over command of the regiments, but the office of captain was likely to be filled either by the already overburdened Justices or by their younger sons who had the time and the zeal but not the experience to organize and command the rough material under them. Staffordshire showed its wisdom in paying its trained band officers £20 a year; elsewhere the situation reached such extremes that gentry refusing to serve as captains were brought before the Privy Council for punishment. The summer muster, which theoretically gathered officers and men of each regiment together for two days' training, must often have been little more than a farce. Many never appeared at all, either through sheer laziness or because the calls of agricultural work, especially if the muster coincided with harvest, naturally took precedence. There was little in the inspection and the drill which followed it to inspire the local militiaman with any fervour for soldiering or to suggest to him that he was needed by his King and country. Yet Charles had begun his self-appointed task of revitalizing the militia in 1626 by sending into the counties experienced soldiers who left their regiments in the Low Countries to spend three months teaching the English yokels how to bear arms. It was an admirable move, but unfortunately the experts' lessons were quickly forgotten, and all too soon the militia, whose lack of sense of purpose was probably the most dangerous thing about it, was allowed to slip back again into an easy carelessness.

There was a brief flurry of activity in 1635 when the Privy Council in its general muster order charged the deputy lieutenants with 'connivance and remissnes of late yeares'. It was only in November 1638, with the threat of almost immediate hostility hanging over them, that King and Council again ordered all the Lord Lieutenants to hold musters in their counties. Early in the spring of 1639 militias from most of the counties north of the Trent gathered to the King at York, but the first Bishops' War ended before it had really begun early that same summer. The deputy lieutenants were not however to be left in peace for long. On 26 March 1640 Charles issued his orders for raising twenty-seven thousand men from the counties of England and Wales. The instructions sounded extremely competent. Weekly exercising was to begin; a county rendez-vous was fixed for 10 May; the men were to be prepared to march north ten days later. But in fact by the time the rendez-vous had been postponed to June money was becoming short, and the civilian opposition to paying coat and conduct money was running the deputy lieutenants into serious difficulties. The constables were only able to bring in small fractions of the sums they were supposed to collect. When the men received no pay they deserted; by the end of June the story from every county was one of mass desertion and vandalism, and the disorders and atrocities only increased as the summer went on. The prisoners in the house of correction at Wakefield were set free by passing troops; the Somerset levies murdered a Roman Catholic officer before deserting homewards; in Derbyshire troops tore down Sir John Coke's palings and set fire to his mill; the Wiltshire soldiers broke open the county gaol to release those committed for not paying coat and conduct money; the Berkshire forces disbanded in Oxfordshire. Throughout the eastern counties troops were breaking into churches and tearing out communion rails and making bonfires of them. Believing that Bishop Matthew Wren, a strong Laudian, was in a Wisbech church, a mob of angry soldiers battered on the doors and windows shouting, 'Give us the damned Bishop of Ely.' [31] The King's army had become an army in open revolt.

The more or less complete breakdown of the militia and the deputy lieutenants between 1630 and 1640 contrasts strikingly with the success of the Justices and local administration during the same period. How was it that one should succeed and the other fail when the same class of men – in very many cases the same individuals – were involved? One might argue that a country squire was better fitted to perform acts of philanthropy towards the poor or execute justice upon petty criminals than to ape a military ardour which did not come naturally to him. But there is more to it than this. The Justice of the Peace, together with his subordinates, was an effective instrument of the central government largely because the central government went to great lengths to perfect him and to keep him up to standard. Supervision by the Council and the pressure of the Judges of Assize was constant and relentless; the development of Petty Sessions saw to it that the individual Justice did not slacken between sessions. Moreover the Council took good care to keep itself informed of the activities of the Justices and it demanded and expected to receive detailed reports of how its orders were being fulfilled. But supervision of the deputy lieutenants lay with the Lord Lieutenant and there was no regular channel by which the Council was kept informed of what was going on. If the Privy Council seemed satisfied with what it knew of the militia during the 1630s this was a satisfaction based on more or less total ignorance.

As always in the history of local government success or failure cannot be measured merely in terms of a smooth-running administrative machine. As in the sixteenth century, the gentry were prepared to serve the Crown loyally when they found its aims coincided reasonably with their own. They respected a campaign to put down vagabonds and masterless men, and they approved of the relief of the poor and even more of setting the poor to work. But they had little sympathy with Charles's disforestation and emparkment, for example, and would do nothing to allay the local opposition to it. The limits of the Justices' actions can be seen clearly enough in the unrest in Wiltshire at the King's violent and extensive enclosures. The Justices and deputy lieutenants moved only with reluctance against the rioters who objected to them. In 1633 the Judges of Assize were informed that the rebels had 'received private encouragement from some gentlemen of quality'. At the revolt at the enclosure of Braydon Forest in 1631 the deputy lieutenants said they could not call out the trained band, and as for 'the bordering justices' they 'are vnwilling to be seene actors in anything against their neighbors'. Charles and the Privy Council could be under no illusion about the support for the rebellions from every rank of society or of the isolation of the government.

We yet vnderstand that thes riotters continue ther former outrages, which could not be if the High shiriff, deputy Lieutenants and Justices of peace, and vnder them the constables and other inferior officers, did in ther seuerall places effectually performe ther duitys, but ther remissnes in executing thes our commands geues incouragement to the inferior sort of people, who are but the actors of thes mischeifs which others of better quality doe vnderhand sett on foot or connyve at.[32]

Charles had had ten years in which to woo the gentry and he had failed abysmally. He had allowed his high ideals of social justice to become overlaid by his desperate search for money, and he had launched himself upon the promotion of ill-conceived financial expedients. The gentry had had to submit to ten years of persistent interference with their purses, and in 1638 it seemed that they were being asked to undertake the heavy trouble and the not inconsiderable expense of making the largest levy of troops within the memory of man – merely 'for a war on their Protestant neighbours and fellow-subjects, provoked by the Archbishop', that is, by Laud.[33] Charles had forgotten Elizabeth's example in dealing with her Justices (though it was possibly an example which he was congenitally incapable of following) which demonstrated that success demanded the maintenance of a delicate equilibrium between the authority of the Crown and the demands of the subject.

Long before the King raised his standard at Nottingham in August 1642 the ranging of parties and the manoeuvres for place were disturbing the normal routine of local government. In the early years of the war regular meeting of Quarter Sessions became difficult, sometimes impossible. A short but vivid note in the

Order Book tells what happened at the Michaelmas Sessions 1642 in Warwickshire. The two Justices who attended had both been in the commission since 1625, and Holt was over seventy.

Note that there was a Quarter Sessions holden at Warwick upon Tuesday next after the feast of St Michael the Archangel 1642, before Sir Thomas Holt, knight and baronet, and John Lisle, esquire (only) who came not to the hall until after one of the clock and within one hour after the lord Rochford entered Warwick with 800 soldiers and the noise of the drums and the trumpets (which came with him) so disturbed the court that the court was instantly adjourned to the Swan, which was so filled with his lordship and his soldiers that nothing could be done there.[34]

Neither of them ever sat again at a Quarter Sessions, and the court was not held in the county for the next three years. The last Quarter Sessions held in Wiltshire was at Trinity 1644, when no more than two Justices appeared and the meeting lasted only one day. After that there is no record of further meetings until Trinity 1646. The same was true, in varying degrees, throughout the country. Out of sessions local government probably continued in a perfunctory and half-hearted manner, though the evidence for this is scanty. In Wiltshire in 1646 it was reported that although there were many Justices on the commission 'very few of them are sworn to execute their offices, whereby His Majesty's service and the service of the country is much hindered'.[35] The defection of lesser officials was equally, if not more, serious. It proved virtually impossible to hold court leets to elect constables, men were thus unable to relinquish their posts, and even if successors were elected they often refused to serve. Everywhere that web of mutual responsibility and duty, the very stuff of successful government, was breaking down: there were hundreds without their constables, parishes without church-wardens.

Naturally enough the execution of the Poor Law suffered during the years of war, and the arrears of contributions to poor relief mounted steadily. The practice of putting the able-bodied to work inevitably ceased since both armies were recruiting every man they could lay their hands on. In Hertfordshire the waggoners were being hired for the Parliamentary army at half a crown a day, exactly twice the sum paid them by the local farmers, so this was an opportunity to be grasped willingly. When the armies disbanded the countryside swarmed again with vagrants and beggars. Various provincial towns built workhouses in which to house the poor, but there is no evidence of the parish officers supplying a stock of flax, hemp, iron and so on, to provide them with work. 'In all England,' wrote Sir Matthew Hale about 1659, 'it is rare to see any provision of a stock in any parish for the relief of the able-bodied poor.'[36] During the Commonwealth there were few innovations in the Poor Law, and indeed the concern of the government seems to have been to ensure the execution of the existing laws. The ordinance of the Lords in 1647 appealed to the Justices because 'by reason of the unhappy distractions of these times the putting of the Lawes into execution have been altogether neglected'.[37] Three years later several resolutions were passed by Parliament and a committee appointed to revive the laws concerning the poor and setting them to work, and 'to consider by what means or default the same are become ineffectual or are not put in execution'.

Meanwhile on the Bench of Justices itself certain changes were taking place among the traditional holders of office, as in the case of the Norfolk Bench. In the first place the Long Parliament secured the exclusion of clergy and diocesan officials as part of its attack on the ecclesiastical hierarchy. Thus the Archdeacon of Norwich, Andrew Byng, one of the translators of the Authorized Version, ceased to be a Justice, as did Clement Corbett, Vicar-General of the Bishop of Norwich. Their places were taken by men more likely to be sympathetic to the Parliamentary cause, successful soldiers such as Cromwell's brother-in-law Valentine Wauton, Governor of King's Lynn; lesser gentry like Luke Constable, an attorney of Swaffham, or Tobias Pedder, constable of the hundred of Hunstanton; town merchants, the mayors of King's Lynn and the bailiffs of Great Yarmouth – all strong supporters of the regime but not quite of the social standing to have gained entry to the commission for the county before the war.[38] The appearance of this new personnel was significant: local government was breaking down in these years because it was so difficult to find enough Justices to support the regime. The basic structure of county government might have changed little in form but the system was not working as efficiently as it had before the war.

To add to this confusion county committees were set up by an ordinance of February 1643, side by side with the continuing though extenuated Quarter Sessions, to raise money for the Parliamentary forces. Inevitably there was a good deal of overlapping of personnel and Justices of Parliamentary sympathies found themselves members of both. Indeed in such a predominantly Parliamentary county as Suffolk the members of the county committee differed little from the same knot of men who had been the local governors of the county for the past decade. From this Suffolk gained a cohesion and stability which was markedly absent elsewhere. In Wiltshire the committee's work was hampered by the severe feuds of two of its leaders, Sir Edward Hungerford and Sir Edward Baynton. In Kent control of the committee passed from the county gentry to others, men of new and unpopular families such as Sir Michael Livesey the regicide, until in 1648 the central knot of county gentry united and rose against them. Their rebellion failed: it was bound to fail before Fairfax and the national armies. But the episode illustrates a recurrent theme of this study: the county gentry, the old-established families, were the best rulers of local society. They and they alone were able to control their localities successfully.

This was made very clear during the years of the Cromwellian interregnum, those eleven years in which Oliver Cromwell and his successor tried in vain to establish a firm government. The reasons for his ultimate failure are complex, but one cause can be deduced from a study of local government at this time: the withdrawal of the old ruling families left the counties in the hands of lesser men unequal to their task and powerless to exert authority in times of such uncertainty and unrest. The only alternative to complete breakdown in such a situation was a centralized military despotism, that is to say the rule of the Major-Generals. The hold of the traditional men and the traditional ways however went deep. There might be a new spirit of moral purpose, expressed so admirably by the Mayor of Salisbury to the Wiltshire Bench: 'God expects you should be faithful to

74

your trust. You are posting to the grave every day, you dwell upon the borders of eternity. How dreadful will a dieinge bed be to a negligent magistrate.'[39] But neither this new spirit nor the sword could eradicate a nation-wide longing for a return to the old forms of county society and county government. Dr Everitt has spoken of 'the far-reaching power of the indigenous clans of the county'. Such men had no special love for the Stuarts, no sentimental attachment to Charles II, but they did long for the way of life to which they had been accustomed: they could not support the proscription of Anglicanism, they loathed the atmosphere of military force, the threat of prying interference into their private lives; they wanted, more than anything else, local stability. Ironically enough it was the very success of Cromwell's policy of centralization which created this craving for a return to the old forms of government whose genius was essentially local. But Cromwell was not prepared to push his social revolution far enough: he had not broken the power of the country gentry and they could not for ever remain excluded from their inherited place at the seat of county government. 'If the Great Rebellion had proved anything it was the necessity of employing country gentry in country affairs.'[40]

References

1. C. Wilson, *England's Apprenticeship 1603–1763*, Longmans, 1965, p. 108.
2. R. H. Tawney's introduction to D. Brunton and D. H. Pennington, *Members of the Long Parliament*, Allen & Unwin, 1954, p. xv.
3. James I's and Charles I's frequent efforts to send gentry back into their counties from London show that a small minority was already London-centred to some degree.
4. A. M. Everitt, *The County Committee of Kent in the Civil War*, Leicester University Occasional Paper, 1957, p. 8.
5. A. M. Everitt, 'Social Mobility in Early Modern England', *Past and Present*, 1966, No. 33, p. 59. The recent interest in the structure of county and local society during this period is a welcome corrective to the emphasis given, by the controversy on the rise or fall of the gentry, to the *individual* member of the gentry taken out of the natural context of his native county.
6. Everitt, *County Committee of Kent*, p. 21.
7. A. M. Everitt, *Suffolk and the Great Rebellion 1640–1660*, Suffolk Record Society, Ipswich, 1960, p. 19.

8. M. C. Cross, 'The third Earl of Huntingdon and Elizabethan Leicestershire', *Leicestershire Archaeological Society Transactions*, 1960, XXXVI.

9. J. H. Plumb, 'Political History of Leicestershire 1530–1885', *V.C.H. Leicestershire*, 1954, II, pp. 109–10.

10. T. G. Barnes, *Somerset 1625–1640: a County's Government during the 'Personal Rule'*, Harvard, Oxford University Press, 1961, p. 296.

11. Tawney, *op. cit.*, p. xvii.

12. *op. cit.*, p. xiv.

13. L. Stone, *The Crisis of the Aristocracy 1558–1641*, Oxford University Press, 1965, p. 223.

14. Barnes, *op. cit.*, p. 282.

15. Wilson, *op. cit.*, pp. 16–17.

16. Quoted E. M. Leonard, *The Early History of Poor Relief*, 1900, p. 242.

17. *ibid.*, p. 243.

18. *ibid.*, p. 147.

19. Barnes, *op. cit.*, p. 178.

20. *ibid.*, p. 180.

21. He was restored in 1637. *ibid.*, p. 186, note 30.

22. Quoted Leonard, *op. cit.*, p. 299.

23. *ibid.*, p. 257.

24. *ibid.*, pp. 261, 251.

25. Barnes, *op. cit.*, p. 81.

26. See pages 44, 61 above.

27. Barnes, *op. cit.*, p. 208.

28. *ibid.*, p. 218.

29. *ibid.*, p. 239.

30. *ibid.*, Chapter IX.

31. C. V. Wedgwood, *The King's Peace 1637–1641*, Collins, 1955, pp. 338–9.

32. E. Kerridge, 'The Revolts in Wiltshire against Charles I', *Wiltshire Archaeological and Natural History Magazine*, 1958, LVII, pp. 64–75.

33. Wedgwood, *op. cit.*, p. 336.

34. *Warwickshire County Records*, eds. S. C. Ratcliff and H. C. Johnson, Stephens, Warwick, 1936, II, pp. 125–6.

35. J. Hurstfield, 'County Government 1530–1660', *V.C.H. Wiltshire*, 1957, V, p. 107.

36. S. and B. Webb, *English Poor Law History*, I, *The Old Poor Law*, 1927, p. 97.

37. Quoted Leonard, *op. cit.*, p. 270.

38. *Norfolk Quarter Sessions Order Book 1650–1657*, Norfolk Record Society, Norwich, ed. D. E. Howell James, 1955, p. 5.

39. Historical Manuscripts Commission, Various Collections, I, p. 132, quoted B. Osborne, *Justices of the Peace*, 1960, p. 121.

40. A. M. Everitt, *The Community of Kent and the Great Rebellion 1640–60*, Leicester University Press, 1966, p. 323, upon whose work the concluding paragraph of this chapter is very largely based.

CHAPTER FOUR

1660–1780
Property and Philanthropy

'THERE exists no privileged order to whom the Statistics of Honour and Dignity exclusively belong, but their Acquirement is Open to All who have energy to pursue them; and this Observation is confirmed by daily instances of Persons raising themselves from the most humble to the most elevated stations, by Means honourable to themselves, and useful to the Community.' So an eighteenth-century Chairman of the Gloucestershire Bench of Justices addressed his fellow magistrates and the assembled court at Quarter Sessions. He saw with a clarity which was by no means usual the peculiar characteristics of English society, and recognized that both society in general and the Bench to which he belonged in particular benefited by this. More common among his contemporaries was an alarmed protest at the entry of new blood into the established ranks. Oliver Goldsmith, that simple and rather muddle-headed conservative, attacked commerce and commercial wealth as disturbers of the social equilibrium, and was suspicious of business as a solvent of the ordered traditional society that was the eighteenth-century ideal. Not that there was anything new in this. Voices had been raised in horrified protest at the influx of commercial and industrial wealth in Elizabethan as they were still to be in Victorian England. There was nothing novel about either the situation itself or the alarm it caused in contemporary onlookers. It was a phenomenon peculiar to English society and one of the sources of its strength, in Parliament as in Quarter Sessions.

Yet the landowners who were believed to be the backbone of the traditional ruling class and who were themselves most vehement in upholding its traditions were often closer to what they appeared to despise than they cared always to remember or admit. It might be that the family fortunes had been founded by no more distant ancestor than a father or a grandfather who had been in trade. Few owners of estates gained all or most of their incomes from agricultural profits; few could with honesty claim no knowledge of business or no connexion with trading circles. This was as true of Members of Parliament as it was of Justices of the Peace. Nothing is more characteristic of the continuity and flexibility of English institutions than this lasting marriage of mercantile and landed wealth.[1] English society in the eighteenth century was not a series of closed castes, nor had it ever been. Always for those who were successful there was little difficulty in improving one's social status. Buying estates, making the right marriage, acquiring a knighthood, holding the office of Sheriff, becoming a Justice and thus gaining a footing in county society: this was a familiar pattern. So the eighteenth-century Bench reflects the social mobility of the age, and a rather closer look at its composition will show that it was not, as both the satirists and the reformers, from Fielding to the Webbs, have tried to insist, merely made up of Squire Western and his fellow Tory landowners.

Yet movement was possible only up to a certain level. Eighteenth-century society was dominated by the aristocracy and though it was saved from anything approaching the rigidity of contemporary European aristocracies by the fact that sons of peers become commoners, the hundred and fifty or so active peers of the early eighteenth century were more aware of their powers and privileges than either their predecessors or successors, and consequently there was a deepening sense of caste among them. The letters of Horace Walpole and Lord Chesterfield were written by men isolated from the rest of society by their fantastic riches. Their conventions, their way of life built up around their vast estates, their incomes – the really *grands seigneurs* like the Dukes of Bedford, Devonshire, Northumberland and so on could claim forty or even fifty thousand pounds per annum – set them apart.[2] Such men naturally dominated their localities, and the Lord Lieutenancy was their perquisite. This gave them a uniquely powerful position, with one foot in London close to the central government, and the other firmly planted in their native county.

The Duke of Newcastle was Lord Lieutenant throughout most of his life of three counties, Sussex, Nottinghamshire and Middlesex, but most peers were content with one. They were able to keep an eye on local appointments, especially entry to the Bench, and it was not difficult to build up a local following when they were in touch with the Court, the centre of all patronage. The Court naturally insisted on loyalty from these magnates, and it was by no means unusual for them to be dismissed from office by the government. The Duke of Bolton held Hampshire, Dorset and Carmarthen, but when he quarrelled with the government in 1733 he was dismissed from all three.[3] The news of impending or threatened loss of office would cause consternation in the counties, for the Lord Lieutenant wielded an immense power among the squirearchy and the lesser landowners; if he were out of office his followers might also find themselves in the desert.

Faction played if anything a greater part in eighteenth-century life than ever before. There were several reasons for this, but the existence of a Parliament that could be counted on to meet regularly every year was the most important one. After 1689 men realizedthat Parliament would no longer depend upon the whim of the King but had become a permanent feature of the constitution. In 1694 the Triennial Bill made a general election certain once in every three years; in 1716 the Septennial Act made it every seven years. As elections became more frequent so did the struggles of the local families to establish their control of the local seats. Election costs soared as landowners vied with each other in lavish entertainment, generous bribes, outright buying of votes. The smaller squires tended to be forced out of the battle: these were contests among the aristocracy and the most prosperous landowners. But few could remain uninvolved. Patronage became more and more the decisive feature in political life and men sold their allegiance to the bidder who offered the best hope of places and rewards. The strife was at its most bitter in the early years of the eighteenth century, and since it was fought out at every level of society naturally enough Quarter Sessions became a focal point for the building up of strong parties. It was because he realized this that Walpole remained a J.P. all his life and took his place on the Bench whenever he was in Norfolk: the tentacles of his power spread over the whole of north-west Norfolk. 'With his strong political realism he knew well enough that the strength of his party rested on the loyalty of his brother justices. Without their tacit consent no political structure could last for long. They were the most vital part of local government.'[4]

In counties where the alignments were still far from settled the prospect of the issue of a new commission of the peace was the signal for plots to begin, and lists and letters began to pass round the county. The gentry were much alarmed at the machinations of the nobility, reported Lord Ducie's spy in 1754, a Justice who had been attending a 'tedious session' at Gloucester in order to discover for his lordship how things were progressing on the Bench. 'There is a good deal of talk and I find a good deal of uneasiness among the Gentlemen at the new Commission,' Lord Ducie wrote to Lord Hardwick, and indeed the atmosphere of secrecy and intrigue must have heightened their fears and misgivings. Ducie's list made it plain whom he thought 'exceptionable' or 'improper', and concluded with 'names of proper persons recommended by my Intelligencers but not insisted upon by me'.[5] Lord Berkeley, who as Lord Lieutenant exercised the greatest possible power on these occasions, suggested that it would be more diplomatic to include some of the opposition party, while promising Ducie that 'he could take care to have a majority on the right side'.

'To say the truth I believe we have descended as Low already in filling up the Commission as is right,' complained George Augustus Selwyn, expressing a fear common among the magistracy. Under the exigencies of political intrigue it seemed that men who were not of socially unimpeachable standards were gaining entry to the Bench. 'Many of them are Persons who are not entitled to such a Trust from their Rank, Fortune or Capacities, so that the list can be calculated only for improper purposes,' was the opinion of a Gloucestershire Justice, James Dutton, in 1754.[6] Yet one may be sure that the pessimism was not altogether justified. The cohesion of county society was such that government rested, as it had always done, primarily with those families whose acres and ancestry gave them the prerogative to be the local governors. For the Civil War and the years that followed had not diminished but rather increased the power of the gentry. 1660 saw a return of the old ruling families of the shire to the local as well as to the national political scene. Their traditional right to rule their counties was a most powerful weapon in the face of which Charles I, then Parliament, and finally Cromwell, had in turn been defeated. It was an act of supreme foolishness on the part of Charles II and James II to attempt to fly in the face of Providence and tamper with this accepted pattern.

The Civil War had increased the growing independence of the Justices, and the Restoration did little to reverse the trend. The Star Chamber, that familiar weapon often wielded by the Crown in the earlier seventeenth century to bring them to heel, was not re-established in 1660. During Charles II's reign the Privy Council appear to have summoned and questioned Justices on occasion but the House of Commons frowned upon this practice and it was dropped. The government turned to the only weapon it could still use to reassert its authority: dismissal from the commission. And it was used, on a large scale, by Charles II from 1680 to 1683, and by James II from 1686 to 1688. A purge early in 1680 dismissed from office many of those who were known to favour excluding the Catholic James from succession to the throne, and in 1681 the axe fell upon Lord Lieutenants and deputy lieutenants. But James II went much further. Determined to gain support for his pro-Roman Catholic policy he appointed a committee of Council in 1686 to revise the magistracy, and in the five months following October 1686 exactly half the Justices in the country were removed from office. He simply replaced all those who would not pledge themselves to support him, above all in the repeal of the Test Act. The country Justices, faced with these insulting demands, naturally showed their mettle and were consequently turned off the Bench in droves.[7]

All but eight of the Cumberland Justices were 'disjusticed', according to the Bishop of Carlisle. In Leicestershire only one Justice was prepared to support James. Injury was added to insult when they found that their place was being taken by Dissenters and Roman Catholics, by men of no property or standing, or by men of such notorious reputation as Robert

Fielding, who when he was put in the commission of Warwickshire for 1685 was already distinguished by having received a pardon for manslaughter in 1677. He subsequently professed conversion to Roman Catholicism in 1687, was imprisoned at Newgate in 1696 accused of assaulting and dangerously wounding a Middlesex J.P., and finally was convicted in 1706 at the Old Bailey of bigamously marrying the Duchess of Cleveland, mistress of Charles II.[8]

Sir John Reresby wrote in alarm to the Duke of Newcastle in November 1688:

In the afternoon we was all surprized by the clerke of the peace comming to supersede Sir Henry Goodrick, Mr Tankard, Sir John Kaye, Sir Michael Wentworth, Sir Thomas Yarbugh, and above twenty more principall gentlemen of this rideing (the most eminent for quality and estates) from being justices of the peace, bringing at the same time another commission wherein severall new ones are put in, and amongst others John Eyre of Sheffield Parke, Mr Ratcliff etc. The first can neither write nor read, the second is a bailiff to the Duchesse Dowagere of Norfolk's rents, and neither of them have one foot of freehould land in England. . . .[9]

Such a violation of the accepted social order brought its inevitable consequences: almost the entire country rejected James and welcomed William III with open arms. The Crown's failure to win support in the localities was not the least of the causes of the Revolution. 1689 brought the issue of new commissions with the familiar names: Guises, Hicks, Masters in Gloucestershire; Walpoles in Norfolk; Onslows and Knatchbulls in Kent; Verneys, Bridgemans and Bromleys in Warwickshire.

But what sort of man was the traditional English country Justice of the eighteenth century? Fielding and Smollett painted their lurid pictures; the *Gentleman's Magazine* expostulated about 'the good-natured fox-hunter who spends his day on horseback, and his evenings eating and drinking'.[10] Macaulay's famous description of the bucolic squire has immortalized the early eighteenth-century Justice and the Webbs have done little to correct the impression with their stereotyped portraits: the Rural Tyrant, the Sycophant Justice, the Mouthpiece of the Clerk. 'To a crucial extent the social supremacy of the landowners rested on their superior education and culture. . . . The landed classes governed the country and led society because they formed an élite, educated and trained from childhood to fulfil their role in society.'[11] Of course there were boors and drunkards among them, those who looked no farther than the hunting-field and the gaming-table. But in general the eighteenth-century squire had been educated well, either at one of the four hundred or so grammar schools or at a public school. On any Bench a considerable number would have gone to university and possibly followed this by a year or two at one of the Inns of Court. And even making the Grand Tour was by no means rare among country squires. Sir George Onesiphorus Paul, the Gloucestershire Justice, was in Europe in 1767–8 and compiled notebooks describing his journeys, his acquaintances and his purchases. Nor did they forget their learning when their formal education was over. A more typical library than that of Macaulay's squire was Paul's, recorded in the inventory of his house. He combined a good foundation of the classics with a representative selection of contemporary French and English literature, from Molière, Beaumarchais, Voltaire and Rousseau to Johnson, Smollett, Fielding, Gibbon and Scott. An interest in economics and politics was represented by Adam Smith, Defoe, Necker, Bolingbroke and Godwin. The Grand Tour had its mementoes in *Le pitture di Bologna* and the *Decamerone di Boccaccio*, while Hogarth's *Analysis of Beauty* and Uvedale Price's studies of the picturesque suggested a continuing interest in the arts. A large section on local government included all the authorities on the office of the Justice of the Peace from Lambarde's *Eirenarcha* to the Rev. Richard Burn's treatise published in Paul's own day, as well as tracts on the duties of Sheriff and constable, and numerous other contemporary pamphlets.[12] The purchase of books and the subscriptions to new publications which figure in the Justices' accounts reveal a wide interest in theology, politics, economics and contemporary affairs. The *Gentleman's Magazine* must have graced the shelves of many a Justice's library. It was not uncommon to find on the Bench a reasonable working knowledge of architecture, for this was considered part of the education of a gentleman, and many took an active part in transforming their seventeenth-century houses into the Palladian mansions demanded by fashionable taste. The antiquarian studies which flourished throughout the eighteenth century drew much of their support from the ranks of the gentry. We know from Sir William Dugdale's diary and correspondence how much his great history of Warwickshire owed to the men who were in the commission of the peace for the county in 1685. It was written for them and reflects their social and intellectual interests.[13]

But it would be false to equate the Bench of Justices with the country squires, though this is an assumption generally made. For the Bench, like English society itself, never became a closed caste but held its door open to men in other walks of life, whether professional, commercial or industrial. The Gloucestershire Bench in the eighteenth century is typical in reflecting every facet of the county it served, which in this case combined agricultural interests in the rich farmlands of the Cotswolds and the Vale of Berkeley with a flourishing textile industry in the Stroud Valley, the mining areas of Kingswood and the Forest of Dean, and whose bounds even included the outskirts of Bristol with all its commercial connexions.[14] An analysis of its personnel makes an interesting picture. The landowners formed the greatest proportion of the Justices, as might be expected. Of these a dozen came of families settled in the county since the Middle Ages, but the majority were of sixteenth- and seventeenth-century origin – twelve from the former, thirteen from the latter – while eleven were newcomers, only settling in the county in the eighteenth century either because they married a local heiress or because they were following the familiar pattern of buying a country estate and settling down to found a county family. The second largest group of Justices were the dozen clothiers from the Stroud Valley clothing district. Ten Bristol merchants sat on the Bench, some of them men who, having made their fortune in trade, bought estates in the county; but even so they did not sever their links with the city and their business connexions there. The professions were represented by two doctors and two barristers. Three J.P.s do not fit easily into any category: Henry Wyatt, a Stroud brewer, John Hollings, a mercer and also a partner in a bank, and Joseph Cripps, a Cirencester banker who was also concerned with carpet manufacture.

The clergy demand rather more detailed description. The numbers of clerical Justices on the Gloucestershire Bench were growing throughout the century until by the 1780s there were fifteen. They were among the most distinguished, both in education and administrative ability. In many cases they were the younger sons of landowners, and in a number of instances they held the family living while an elder brother was squire of the village. As many as five families at this time had brothers, one lay and one clerical, on the Bench, and there was little or nothing to distinguish the clerics from the landowners. But in many cases the clergy, presented to their livings by the Crown or their old colleges, came from outside the county itself and represented an influx of new blood and connexions with other parts of the country. Thus some came from places as remote from Gloucestershire as Cumberland, Suffolk or Devon, while in the social scale they ranged from the son of a 'pleb' to the son of a judge and the grandson of a bishop. A number held livings in plurality in neighbouring dioceses, and several held ecclesiastical offices in cathedrals as distant as York and Exeter. The diaries of two of them show how impossible it is to make any generalization about the clerical Justice.

We have a picture of one country parson from his own pen, *A Narrative of the life of the Rev. Charles Coxwell M.A. written by Himself.* It is a record of parochial duties and simple hobbies.

He passed with peculiar pleasure the time which he devoted to the reading of the Scriptures or to other useful Learning in his study; and a Turn for Mechanics afforded him at proper sessions no small Amusement in his Laboratory. He was never fond of Cards; though he would sometimes join with his Friends and Family at playing them but chose rather when he could be excused, to dedicate his Evening Hours to Reading and Improvement of his Mind. Being but a timid Rider, he declined the Exercise of Hunting, tho' situated in the Neighbourhood of Hounds; but was fond of Shooting, albeit he was a very indifferent Marksman as being near-sighted and obliged to make use of Glasses. He had some knowledge of Music and performed but poorly on the Violin; having never had the benefit of any regular instruction nor opportunities of playing in Concert through his Residence in a Country Village.

The diary of Henry Gorges Dobyns Yate presents a very different life.[15] Being a clergyman of a higher social standing he moved in more exalted circles. He was generally absent from his parish for two months or more in the year. In 1786 he visited London and York; the following year he was in London, working in the British Museum and attending debates at the House of Commons; another year he spent the months of May and June in Malvern. His friends included several members of the aristocracy. Yet he did not neglect his parochial duties. His family were the lords of the manor and the church was partly rebuilt by his brother during his incumbency. He revived the custom of perambulating the bounds, he attended tithe dinners and gave entertainment to the landholders in the parish, and was active in meetings about turnpikes, canals and militia as well as his routine Justice business. A comparable study has not yet been made of any other county, but the general picture would doubtless be similar. In Wiltshire, for example, another west of England cloth-making area, the clothiers took their seats with the gentry and members of the local dynasties, while here too the number of clerical Justices showed a steady increase throughout the century.[16]

The foregoing analysis of the composition of an eighteenth-century Bench will have been misleading if it suggests in any way that the Justices were themselves conscious of belonging to any particular category, or that barriers of class or interest divided them. Most of the Gloucestershire landowners had an investment in some sort of industrial undertaking, iron-works in the Forest of Dean, coal in Kingswood, a local brick-making enterprise and so on. On the other hand those clothiers who were becoming prosperous combined supervision of their mills with the activities of a country gentleman. It seemed quite natural that when a masque was being performed to celebrate the coming of age of Lord Dursley the names of local clothiers should figure in the cast. The bonds that held local society together were strong. To a large extent any county in the early and middle years of the eighteenth century still lived a more or less self-sufficient life, to which the petty personal and social gossip of contemporary correspondence, with its record of hunts and race-meetings, concerts and balls, gives witness. The country houses of the local aristocracy, when they were at home, saw a constant stream of visitors and clients coming to discuss politics, business and county affairs. Educated together (the names on the registers of the local grammar school often included the sons of landowners, clergy, clothiers and merchants, many of whom later sat together on the Bench)[17] and later allied by marriage, meeting frequently in the round of county business and county gaieties, it is scarcely surprising that on finding themselves exiled in London the county gentry should dine together and found a 'County Society'. The verses sung at the first Cumberland dinner in London in 1777[18] show a very real provincial patriotism:

> What though we have els'where found skies more serene
> Yet something we owe to our atmosphere keen;
> Our minds, like our bodies, are vig'rous and hence,
> That boast of our countrie, strong masculine sense.

Life in one's home county could still be rich and varied, and despite the growing attactions of London or Bath, or later in the century Brighton, the countryside still offered many diversions. London in any case was almost ruinously expensive for a country squire who wished to have his family with him, as Sir Thomas Chester, Justice and at that time M.P. for Gloucestershire, found when he set out with his wife and servants in January 1734/5. The lodgings cost him four guineas a week, and the total expenses of his four months' residence came to £371 for lodgings and housekeeping, with a further £384 to meet the bills for clothes and such items as wine (£51), butcher (£31), coal (£15) and candles (£4 14s.).[19] Most preferred to spend the winter months at home, not only for the negative reasons of appalling roads and the discomforts of travel, but because of the attractions the county provided. Fox-hunting grew in popularity throughout the century, and was a sport followed by any who cared to do so, from dukes to small farmers.[20] Horse-racing was equally popular and equally democratic: gentry and farmers as well as members of the aristocracy took their horses to the local race-meetings. Some Justices, like Sir George Onesiphorus Paul, kept their own racing-stables. Wrestling and cock-fighting were other country sports which drew their support from all walks of life. A Nottingham-shire J.P., Sir Thomas Parkyns, was himself a prize-wrestler and author of a book on the subject.[21]

One thing all eighteenth-century Justices shared, whatever the origins of their wealth: a serious, frequently an expert, interest in the management of their estates. They experimented with new machinery, received the latest communications on agricultural improvements from the Board of Agriculture, attended meetings of the local agricultural societies. 'My Chief Employment,' as one of them put it, 'is to improve my little Farm.' But the sense of property was tempered by a sense of philanthropy. The Rev. Thomas Leigh's concern over the enclosure of the Cotswold living of Adlestrop shows this duality; he was anxious that the property should be handed on in the best possible condition for future generations 'so that when my Nephew comes of age it will be ready to hand', but his final care was to leave a couple of acres in case cottages had to be replaced, and to ensure that these should be available for their tenants. Property and paternalism may indeed be taken as themes of the eighteenth-century Bench. Property, its exploitation and its protection, determined the atti-tudes of the Justices on many current problems, and was respon-sible, among other things, for some of the harsher and more unlovely aspects of local government of the period. But paternal-ism softened the rigour of the laws written in the statute book and eased the relations of the local governors with those under their rule.

For many of these Justices Quarter Sessions was a popular meeting where business was lightened by two or three days of conviviality and gossip. 'Our old talking-shop', was how one eighteenth-century Justice referred to it, with a note of warmth. Numbers on the Bench rose greatly during the century. At the end of the seventeenth century in Warwickshire about ten Justices generally attended the Quarter Sessions out of a working body of twenty or so.[22] In Gloucestershire during the 1780s attendance averaged seventeen, and in the last decade of the century had risen to twenty. Both these are large counties, but the figures reflect a trend that was general throughout the country. Numbers were definitely higher than those that the Webbs considered normal. 'Right down to the last quarter of the 18th century,' they write, 'it was evidently unusual for the Bench at quarter sessions to consist of more than three or four magistrates. . . . All the evidence in fact goes to show that the assembly was neither large nor imposing.'[23] But now more routine business than ever was done at Petty Sessions or at organized monthly meetings. The Justices of Kent were meeting regularly in the early years of the eighteenth century in a fixed place on a regular day each month with a clerk. Of other counties much less is known because few minutes of these early meetings have survived.[24] The Rev. Francis Welles, who was an active Justice in Gloucestershire for forty years between 1715 and 1756, kept a very careful diary of his life as a magistrate, dividing every page into two, and devoting one column to his work at Petty Sessions. Unfortunately his nineteenth-century editor dismissed this as of little account and merely summarized it by saying that it was chiefly concerned with disputes between husbandmen and labourers, differences between masters and apprentices, the correction of wayward servants and the removal of paupers. When Gloucestershire built its new houses of correction in the 1780s the plans included a committee room which was to be used for Petty Sessions. Elsewhere proceedings were less formal and the magistrates met at some well-recognized local inn. 'There is a very neat inn at Kingscote,' the Rev. William Lloyd Baker told the collector of excise, 'which I believe I have pointed out to you as the place where most of the meetings of the Gentlemen in this neighbourhood are held.'[25]

By an Act of 1753 'Brewster Sessions' were to be held every September for the licensing of alehouses; the conditions under which licences might be granted were altered from time to time by Quarter Sessions. Here the Justices addressed a great crowd of local publicans, binding them to good behaviour as they renewed their annual licences. For the alehousekeeper was a tough customer, and keeping any sort of control over him was one of the most serious problems facing the local magistrate. As one Gloucestershire Justice who lived near the Stroudwater textile area explained, 'You know that where the lower class of people can get the money they will spend it in liquor, and play off every manoeuvre to check the laws', the danger lying not so much in drunkenness itself as in 'the riotous and illegal meetings held at these small beerhouses'. The magistrates and the squirearchy in general abhorred them the more because they supposedly increased pauperism, and for this reason all the alehouses in Kingswood were suppressed by the Wiltshire Justices in 1677 at the request of the lord of the manor. They were suspected too of encouraging the spread of subversive opinions and promoting propaganda, especially after the Exclusion crisis, and the Grand Jury of Wiltshire asked Quarter Sessions to order that in future a certificate of conformity to the church must be produced before a licence was granted.[26]

In spite of the development of Petty Sessions, and of licensing sessions, a great deal of magistrate's business was still done by the individual Justice acting on his own, in his front parlour, or 'Justice Room', as it is still known today in some country houses. Some Justices indeed seem to have put this side of their duty first, content to be active within their own particular district without ever joining their fellow magistrates at Quarter Sessions at all regularly. A vivid idea of this type of magistrate comes from the notebook kept by Sir William Bromley, a Warwickshire Justice, in the last years of the seventeenth century. High church-man and High Tory, he was described by Robert Harley in 1696 as a 'person of so great reading, good sense and well-poised judgement'. Fresh from the Grand Tour he was elected M.P. for his native county, a seat which he held until becoming M.P. for the University of Oxford in 1700. In 1710 he became Speaker; in 1713 Secretary of State. Yet whenever he was resident at Bagington, his country seat, he took his duties as a Justice seriously, and though not often able to attend Quarter Sessions he threw himself vigorously into the day-to-day affairs of local government in his immediate hundred. He kept a careful notebook of his out-of-sessions business, dealing with the succession of petty crimes and misdemeanours of his neighbourhood:[27]

1691. 7 Feb. On the complaint of — Norton of Kenelworth, mercer, that his daughter Sarah lives an idle, disorderly life and pilfers his goods. Sir W. Boughton and I committed her to the house of correction.

1691. 8 May. Alexander Barlow of Brincklow, alehousekeeper, swore the peace against Gervase Ledgely of the same, carpenter, for beating him and threatening to burn his house.

1691. 3 June. Deposition of John Busbey of Bubnill, husbandman, that on 21 May, being Ascension Day, he saw Henry Robinson, Thomas Adkins and Moses Robinson, pulling the bark off a tree in Spring Wood, belonging to mr. Woodward in Bubnill. Earlier he had seen Henry Robinson with wood he believes was cut from Woodward's property. On examination all confessed. Adkins and Moses Robinson each to pay 3d damages and a 1s fine to the poor; Henry Robinson 6d damages and 2s to the poor.

1691. Martha Nodington, Jane wife of Thomas Dunne, and the wife of Nicholas Bott, all of Kenelworth, were convict on their confessions of selling ale without licence and punished as the statute 3 Car. I directs.

The amount of work that fell to any one individual varied immensely, duties being shared among many in an agreeable part of the country, thickly populated with gentlemen's seats, but in those rural industrial areas or mining areas where Justices were few upon the ground resting all on the shoulders of one man. Thus one Gloucestershire clothier was the only Justice for 60,000 in the Stroudwater Valley, where fluctuations in the domestic cloth industry made riot and unrest almost endemic, and where the arm of the law was most desperately needed. If a magistrate had to be summoned ten miles to read the Riot Act the chances were that by then the disturbance would have grown seriously out of hand. But, by the very nature of the case, no remedy could be found for this unsatisfactory situation. It was the price to be paid for dependence upon the unpaid country gentleman.

Some Justices lightened their burden by employing a clerk, a man that it was only too easy for the contemporary satirists to paint as a heartless scoundrel:

> He, where no Fees his sordid Pen invite,
> Sports with their Tears, too indolent to write;
> Like the fed Monkey in the Fable, vain
> To hear more helpless Animals complain.[28]

In an attempt to safeguard these 'more helpless Animals' the Benches began to draw up tables of fees which clerks might take, and this practice became general by an Act of Parliament in 1753 which ordered that the schedules should be submitted to the Assize Judges for confirmation.[29] The list is long: sixpences, shillings and half crowns were demanded for warrants of summons, for information taken in writing, for examinations of pauper settlements, for warrants of hue and cry ... But it is difficult to know how far these were observed, for the clerk proves an elusive figure. Some bills or papers still survive, but on the whole he remains anonymous. Sometimes a group of Justices would share a clerk between them; sometimes a Justice would manage without clerical help, and either pocket the fees or, like the Rev. Charles Jasper Selwyn, put them to better account. 'Whatever cash may happen to remain in the fund which I call my Sunday school fund, and which has arisen from, and does arise from fees of Justice business,' he decreed in his will of 1794, 'I have appropriated to the benefit of the Sunday schools in Blockley.'

The out-of-sessions side of the Justices' work grew during the eighteenth century more than ever before as it fell to them to deal with the coming of the turnpikes, the levying of land-tax and the enclosure movement in addition to all their other duties. A study of the turnpike trusts alone shows that practically every Justice served on one at least. Attendance at the meetings often involved them in travelling long distances, and the trustees were expected to defray their own expenses. One Gloucestershire Justice who was for forty-six years the trustee of his local turnpike kept its accounts meticulously, recording the quarterly meetings, the repairs to gates and toll-houses, the yearly auction of the tolls. The latter at least was a social occasion for which he noted the payment of 13s. 'for 3 Bowls of Punch to encourage the Bidders for the tolls, many attending for that purpose'. The diary or correspondence of any conscientious eighteenth-century landowner is full of the many claims made upon his time and energies. Ralph Ward of Gisborough, for example, in the middle years of the century would attend meetings about an enclosure that stretched on for months until all parties were satisfied, or as highway commissioner would ride out on to the moors to supervise the work of road and bridge-building, often meeting his fellow commissioners at nine in the morning and not getting home until four or even later. 'Went to the Highways,' runs a characteristic entry in his journal, 'where we had 8 or 10 carts loading stones and gravel where we put in a Gantree or Bridge against Cook's ground in Yarm Lane. Where I attended the whole day till near 6 without meat or drink, save a little water. Ye work was done to my satisfaction.'[30]

One Gloucestershire Justice reckoned that the greater part of his mornings was taken up in settling Poor Law disputes. This admittedly was in 1800 when the weight of Poor Law business was at its greatest, but the sentiment might well have been expressed at any time throughout this period. As always, whether at Quarter Sessions, Petty Sessions or in his own home, the problem which confronted any Justice most insistently was that of 'the poor'. An analysis of the numbers of poor in one county may clarify the size and urgency of that problem. The occasional tax assessments which affected the entire population of the country throw a sudden gleam of light on otherwise submerged and forgotten areas of society. The hearth tax returns of 1670 show that poverty and near-poverty were as conspicuous in the Leicestershire villages at the end of the seventeenth century as they had been in Tudor times. In 1524 households dependent wholly or in part upon wage labour formed 30 per cent of the total; the same proportion were in 1670 deemed too poor to pay hearth tax. West Goscote, a region of poor soil and highly developed industry, showed the highest figure, 36·5 per cent, but Framland, with its rich farming land, still registered 25 per cent. In the county as a whole the proportion of poor households was 31 per cent: thus one in every three families lived in poverty or destitution.[31]

Between 1660 and 1834 the only alteration of any significance in the Elizabethan Poor Law was made in 1662 by the Act of Settlement and Removal, the main provision of which was that anyone likely to become chargeable to the poor rates was to be forcibly removed back to his 'parish of settlement', generally his birthplace. It is an Act which has come in for a good deal of censure. The Webbs say that it 'spasmodically and irritatingly oppressed the poor and greatly perplexed all the officials concerned'.[32] It has generally been taken to mark the beginning of a harsher attitude towards poverty and to have brought hardship to individuals and detriment to the general economic development of the country by restricting the mobility of labour. In fact, as Professor Wilson shows,[33] the preamble to the statute makes it clear that it arose from the unequal provision made for paupers by the parishes, since those who managed their affairs well drew away the distressed from the parishes which were known to be less generous.[34] Its main purpose was to lessen the administrative difficulties which faced Poor Law officials. Although it was undoubtedly responsible for some cases of individual hardship it was not enforced as rigidly as it might have been, and the population of the countryside was by no means totally immobilized.[35] Only a small proportion of the poor were actually removed, and to many the law did not apply: labourers on the tramp, the migratory Irish, those actually travelling from one town to another looking for a job. A practice became widespread by which parish officers with the consent of two Justices would grant certificates or testimonials allowing their own settled labourers and their families to move elsewhere in search of work and promising to take them back should they become chargeable in their new place of abode.[36] Removal cases were so expensive that the overseer would not involve his parish in them without good reason. And yet a sufficient number of persons were removed annually for these disputes to be one of the most frequent items of Quarter Sessions business, and the appeals often became so complicated that they had to be left for the Judges of Assize to unravel. The Judges at the Nottinghamshire Assizes commented upon the wretched man sent from Plumtree to Burton and then passed on by Burton to Tollerton in the early eighteenth century that 'though Tollerton had no manner or right to the Person, the Justices cannot send him back to Plumtree, but it is a Misfortune upon the parish unless they can find some other Legall Settlement elsewhere', as broad a hint as one could hope for to foist him upon yet another parish.[37] Even the Judges it seems were not immune from this tendency to an irresponsible carelessness which felt that so long as a man was removed it did not greatly matter where.

The easiest way to relieve the poor legally settled within any parish was to give them a small regular money dole, and from this evolved a parish pensions list of weekly payments. Certain parishes preferred to give clothing, coal, allowances of bread and beer, and so on, but this relief in kind was not so common. In fact the money or goods were never enough to live on and the overseers intended that its recipients should make it up by casual labour. Many parishes still maintained a poorhouse during the period, one or two cottages used indiscriminately for the sick, destitute wanderers, paupers and homeless, offering shelter only with no provision of food and no discipline or supervision. It amounted in fact to little more than a place of free lodging, and while it might be more often adequate in a small parish it was likely to prove disastrous in a populous district when it had to hold fifty or more. Workhouses were often little better. For one common failing characterizes the many different workhouses which proliferated during the eighteenth century: whatever the special design or purpose for which they were founded, whether education, gainful employment, medical treatment, or attention to one class of paupers alone, they soon degenerated into the general workhouse indiscriminately housing and maintaining all destitute persons, irrespective of age, sex or condition.

The most optimistic were those which set out to employ the poor profitably. For it seemed clear to contemporaries that a vast supply of labour was lying unexploited because it was idle and untrained. The obvious answer was to compel the poor to work.[38] One of the earliest preachers of this gospel was John Cary who opened a workhouse in Bristol in 1696 where the poor might be employed and their potential labour put to productive uses, ensuring at once that they could be maintained without disorder and used to increase the national wealth. Within the next fifteen years thirteen other towns had followed his example and obtained Local Acts to enable them to establish similar institutions. But before long their hopes were dashed. It proved actually more expensive to maintain the poor with wages in the workhouse than to give them doles as outdoor relief. So the original schemes were soon abandoned in favour of simply giving the able-bodied pauper relief in a form which he did not like, with the automatic result of reducing the number of applicants. To encourage the spread of this system a general Act was passed in 1723 by which parish officers were able to hire premises and maintain them as workhouses. Later Acts allowed parishes to join together for this purpose, and probably between one and two hundred were established.

In the mid 1750s there was a resurgence of the enthusiasm for putting the poor to work. A 'house of industry' was established at Nacton in Suffolk and the precedent followed vigorously elsewhere in East Anglia. These houses were in effect small factories in which the inmates spun wool for the Norwich weavers, knitted stockings, made sacks or fishing-nets. These, claimed a pamphlet of 1761, rendered useful 'many children who otherwise would have figured nowhere but in a landscape of Gainsborough's, the spawn of gipsies, lying upon a sunny bank half naked, with their bundles of stolen wood by their sides. . . .'[39] But again the optimism proved unjustified. The government of these institutions lay with that indeterminate and unwieldy body, the Incorporated Guardians of the Poor, made up of all the J.P.s within the district, all rectors and curates, together with certain freeholders and leaseholders. The Justices were still responsible for supervising all Poor Law administration and for checking their accounts, but in practice they found themselves superseded: the elected acting guardians took over the whole administration of the Poor Law while the management of the house of industry lay with a master or governor paid an annual salary of £40, a sum unlikely to attract applicants of much standing. Before long the experiment began to break down: fraud and embezzlement were common since there was no regular account-keeping and no audit. As it became difficult to sustain the profits of manufacture the governors slipped back, almost without noticing it, into the old ways of indiscriminate relief, until by the end of the century outdoor relief had become more common than indoor maintenance.

Gilbert's Act of 1782 was the last constructive attempt to get the Poor Law out of the hands of overseers. It allowed for the union of parishes to build workhouses for all except the ablebodied. In fact very few parishes took advantage of this: by 1830 only sixty-seven unions had been formed. Nor was the administration of these workhouses when established much better than that of the old overseers. All too soon they became more or less indistinguishable from the old type of workhouse. But Gilbert's Act did encourage the feeling, which was steadily growing by the end of the century, that the unemployed labourer should not be relegated to the workhouse but should be supported by out-door relief.

Thus there was no real coherence in Poor Law policy up to 1780. It was left to fifteen hundred or so parishes and townships to relieve or neglect their own poor, and to adopt out of a variety of expedients whatever best suited their circumstances. This was the fundamental weakness of eighteenth-century poor relief: the total inadequacy of the administrative machinery which set out to deal with a problem of this magnitude. The parish was too small and too feeble to take effective action, and the parish over-seers unfitted for such responsibility. This particular weakness was emphasized by the Act of 1662 which actively encouraged inter-parochial jealousies and squabbles, and inhibited the organization of action on any larger scale. The intention of the legislators to provide work and not maintenance introduced a system too complicated for untrained amateurs who in any case generally held office for only a short period of time. The result was that the rates were heavy and the results small. The whole system became notorious since the overseers tended to regard everything from a financial point of view and to be concerned first and foremost with their own and their neighbours' pockets, and secondly with the human beings who came before them. The harvest of pauperism which they reaped by the end of the century was unfortunate but in many ways inevitable.

There is nothing very edifying about the administration of the Poor Law in the period 1660–1780, although Keir is perhaps rather too harsh in his judgement that 'in the operation of this whole irregular and ill-conceived plan from which every vestige of Tudor and Stuart paternalism was vanishing . . . the work of the eighteenth-century Justice is seen in its least favourable aspect'.[40] Obviously the overseers were the immediate agents for its execution but it is difficult to excuse the Justices from ultimate responsibility. The most that can be said is that, both on and off the Bench, the Justices interposed between the parish overseer and his helpless victim. The letter of the law was greatly mitigated in practice. Individual acts of philanthropy are legion and to inquire to what extent they were prompted by self-interest seems unnecessarily cynical. They were all part of the contemporary view of society and the element of conscious benevolence sometimes makes it hard for the twentieth-century critic to recognize the very genuine warmth and concern underlying them. The owners of property were naturally anxious to instil into the poor and property-less the virtues of 'decorum, industry and subordination'. They thundered against the sins of idleness and praised the 'habits of industry and attention'. But even if they relegated the lower classes to an inferior station they still regarded them as human beings. 'Visit the Cottages of the Poor,' commanded the chairman of one Quarter Sessions, 'and by gentle modes of persuasion inculcate the necessity of sobriety, diligence, neatness and cleanliness, together with an economical management of the little earnings they obtain ... and in this way will be established a firm and compact union between the different classes of society.'[41]

This type of paternalism came naturally to the patriarchal landowner in his dealings with his tenantry or the villages of his immediate neighbourhood. But paternalism as an abstract ideal on the part of the state was by no means dead. The heart might have gone out of the Tudor planned economy as a whole by 1660, but the idea of a paternalistic state protecting the individual persisted, and was appealed to by both the magistracy and the poor throughout the eighteenth century, especially at any times of emergency and more particularly during any corn crisis. Then the regulations for marketing, the action taken against forestalling and regrating, the testing of weights, the licensing of dealers and so on, were put into force, reflecting that traditional attitude which suspected the middleman, wanted to keep marketing as direct as possible, and liked to think of millers and bakers as servants of the community. The Privy Council at such times could and did strengthen the hands of the Justices by issuing proclamations to deal with the recalcitrant, though the 1772 Act which withdrew forestalling was so badly drafted that prosecutions at Quarter Sessions continued until 1800. Yet both the central and local governments recognized change and approved of economic freedom: the two ideals subsisted side by side. Wages for example were rated annually at Quarter Sessions in most counties until about the 1730s when the assessments were quietly dropped. The workers, conservative by nature, looked for security in the retention of all the old statutes regulating conditions of work, and in the west of England textile industry they were fighting in 1756 for the last assessment of wages made by Quarter Sessions in 1728. They actually obtained an Act in 1757 to restore the rating of wages, but it was never put into force by the Bench, due largely to the presence of the clothiers, and in spite of rioting sufficiently severe to require the presence of the military the Act was repealed in the following year and the idea of *laissez-faire* in regard to wages was never again challenged.

For there was within the magistracy an ambivalence of which they themselves were perhaps not fully aware. On the one hand they enjoyed their patriarchal role as guardians of the less fortunate in society and they would want to protect the well-being of the workers. On the other hand, as landowners and clothiers, they recognized that outmoded legislation would not help their own economic interests and what they needed was freedom to experiment and to expand. The working solution they found seems to have been to forward the rights of property, of whatever nature, and at the same time to ease any hardships that this might mean to the labouring classes by individual acts of benevolence, piety, philanthropy. For the time being it served well enough: but before long humanitarian feelings to be effective would have to move on from the era of the gracious bestowing of soup and coals to combating social evils on a rather wider scale.

References

1. C. Wilson, *England's Apprenticeship 1603–1763*, 1965, p. 10.
2. G. E. Mingay, *English Landed Society in the Eighteenth Century*, Routledge, 1963, p. 20.
3. J. H. Plumb, *Sir Robert Walpole: The Making of a Statesman*, Cresset Press, 1956, p. 43.
4. *ibid.*, pp. 46–7.
5. British Museum Add. Mss. 35,604 f. 189.

6. British Museum Add. Mss. 36,601 f. 145.

7. J. P. Kenyon, *The Stuart Constitution 1603–1688. Documents and Commentary*, Cambridge University Press, 1966, pp. 495–6.

8. *Warwickshire County Records*, eds. S. C. Ratcliff and H. C. Johnson, Stephens, Warwick, 1936, ii, pp. xxv–vi.

9. Plumb, *op. cit.*, p. 41.

10. *Gentleman's Magazine*, 1788, p. 315, quoted by S. and B. Webb, *The Parish and the County*, 1906, i, p. 346.

11. Mingay, *op. cit.*, p. 131.

12. See Esther Moir, 'Sir George Onesiphorus Paul', *Gloucestershire Studies*, ed. H. P. R. Finberg, Leicester University Press, 1957, pp. 196–7.

13. *Warwickshire County Records*, eds. S. C. Ratcliff and H. C. Johnson, 1953, viii, p. xxxvii.

14. See Esther Moir, *Local Government in Gloucestershire, 1775–1800, A Study of the Justices of the Peace*, Bristol and Gloucestershire Archaeological Society Records Series, 1969.

15. Gloucestershire Records Office, PE. 85.

16. W. R. Ward, 'County Government 1660–1835', *V.C.H. Wiltshire*, 1957, v, p. 176.

17. This is certainly true of the King's School, Gloucester. I am grateful to the Dean and Chapter for permission to see their register.

18. E. Hughes, *North Country Life in the Eighteenth Century*, II, *Cumberland and Westmorland 1700–1830*, Oxford University Press, 1965, p. 27.

19. Mingay, *op. cit.*, p. 157. A late seventeenth-century estimate gives £800 as the average annual income of knights, and £1,200 of baronets. Even allowing for some increase by this date it is clear how heavily such expenses would weigh in any normal budget. See Mingay, *ibid.*, pp. 22–3.

20. See discussion in the following chapter.

21. Parkyns was a man of parts, the enthusiastic, not to say exuberant, eighteenth-century Justice at his best. See J. D. Chambers, *Nottinghamshire in the Eighteenth Century*, 1932, 2nd edn Cass, 1966, p. 68.

22. *Warwickshire County Records*, eds. H. C. Johnson and N. J. Williams, 1964, ix, p. xx.

23. *op. cit.*, p. 122. A study of the Estreats of Fines in the Public Record Office for 1795 gives some idea of the relative size of the Benches at this date. Middlesex had an average attendance of fifty J.P.s per session, then follow Surrey and Essex with twenty-five each, Devon nineteen, Shropshire eighteen, Kent seventeen and Herefordshire sixteen. Somerset, Northamptonshire, Oxfordshire, Buckinghamshire, Hertfordshire, Worcestershire, Leicestershire, Berkshire, Dorset, Warwickshire and Monmouthshire had between ten and fifteen. The smallest Benches were those with constant adjournments. In Lincolnshire for example Lindsey had six and Holland three; there were generally six at the Suffolk adjournments and from four to seven for those in Nottinghamshire.

24. For the available evidence, see Chambers, *op. cit.*, pp. 52–3; P. Styles,

Development of County Administration in the late XVIIth and early XIXth centuries, illustrated by the Records of the Warwickshire Court of Quarter Sessions 1773–1837, Dugdale Society Occasional Papers, Oxford, 1934, p. 28.

25. Lloyd Baker family papers. I am grateful to Miss Olive Lloyd-Baker of Hardwicke Court, Gloucestershire, for allowing me to see them.

26. Ward, *op. cit.*, v, p. 183. For a description of a disorderly alehouse suppressed by a magistrate see *Hertfordshire County Records,* ed. W. J. Hardy, 1905, VII, p. 141.

27. *Warwickshire County Records*, eds. H. C. Johnson and N. J. Williams, 1964, IX, pp. xxxviii–xl.

28. Langhorne, *The County Justice, A Poem*, 1784, pp. 11–12.

29. Gloucestershire was the first county to settle a table of fees in 1717; Devon ordered a similar table in 1737. See Webbs, *op. cit.*, p. 416, note 2.

30. E. Hughes, *North Country Life in the Eighteenth Century*, I, *The North East*, Oxford University Press, 1952, p. 72.

31. J. Thirsk, 'Agricultural History 1540–1950', *Leicestershire V.C.H.*, 1954, II, p. 228.

32. *English Poor Law History*, I, *The Old Poor Law*, 1927, p. 150, note 2.

33. *op. cit.*, p. 349.

34. This the Webbs for some reason refused to recognize. They dismissed the preamble to the Act as a 'classic piece of legislative mendacity' (p. 325) and devoted the rest of their chapter on the subject to castigating the government for its hardness of heart in creating this 'cruel and costly instrument of tyranny and arbitrary oppression of the wage-earning class'. *The Old Poor Law*, p. 327.

35. See E. M. Hampson, *The Treatment of Poverty in Cambridgeshire*, Cambridge University Press, pp. 126, 267.

36. D. Marshall, *The English Poor in the Eighteenth Century*, Routledge, 1926, pp. 175–6.

37. Chambers, *op. cit.*, p. 263.

38. Another school of thought believed in the education of the poor. The pros and cons of charity schools were being hotly debated at this time and hundreds of benefactors were establishing schools. See M. G. Jones, *The Charity School Movement*, Cass, 1938.

39. Webbs, *The Old Poor Law*, p. 127.

40. D. L. Keir, *Constitutional History of Modern Britain since 1485*, Black, 7th edn, 1964, p. 313.

41. *Charges delivered to the Grand Jury 1798–1804*, by the Rev. John Foley.

CHAPTER FIVE

1780–1834
Reform, Moral and Practical

'BY the beginning of the nineteenth century virtue was advancing on a broad invincible front,' writes G. M. Young.[1] In a well-chosen phrase Asa Briggs has called the years from 1784 to 1867 'the age of improvement'. The growing Victorian moral earnestness, of which the awakened conscience of the later eighteenth century had been the herald, demanded improvement in all spheres of life, secular as well as religious, public as well as private. It was a complex movement compounded of many different impulses, but two of its most characteristic aspects were a desire for efficiency and an urge towards humanitarian reform. The extent to which these interacted one upon the other may be seen in the Clapham Sect, that small select group of middle-class Evangelicals of which Wilberforce was the nucleus and which was very much the product of these years. Their faith was a far different thing from that exuberant revivalism of the earlier eighteenth century, which had been an affair of the heart rather than the mind, and which had emphasized individual conversion and the forgiveness of sins. In the first place the Clapham Sect was the province of men of property and money, its instinctive tendency being to model itself upon 'men of business' according to the eighteenth-century usage of that term, meaning not merely traders but enterprising men throughout society who took themselves and their work seriously, who gave to their calling, whatever it might be, a close and devoted attention, and who showed what we should call a professional concern to make their knowledge do work in the world.[2] The methods they employed were those of an efficient organization: public meetings, voluntary associations, periodicals, for they aimed at reaching and shaping an intelligent public opinion.

This is unmistakably the ethos of professional men using professional methods to promote their ends. That those ends should be moral is also characteristic. The professional ideal, as Edmund Bertram described it in *Mansfield Park*, relied upon laboured dedication to a calling, earnestness and respectability.[3] But younger sons, like Bertram himself, had always gone into the professions. What was new was that the professional ethos was now reaching other ranks of society. By the following century J. S. Mill was to write, 'the country gentleman of the nineteenth century is an administrator and a scientific man. The change may be seen in all its startling clearness amongst the ranks of the aristocracy where often one generation alone was sufficient to make the change from the eighteenth century dilettante, connoisseur, or collector to the careful and informed manager of landed property.'[4]

But even to recognize this 'professionalization' is not yet to reach the real roots of the change that was coming upon English society. In every age men will say that society is changing and for the worse. Contemporaries always see a threat in the increase of the poor and the invasion of landed privilege by new wealth. Cobbett, for example, was sure that there had been a mass movement of new families like the Peels into the landed classes. 'There was much melodrama in Cobbett's sociology,' writes David Spring.[5] Yet for once there was a very considerable element of truth in the observations of the onlookers, though the far-reaching effects of what was taking place were naturally beyond their comprehension. For something even more radical was happening than the coming of a new rich and a new poor. The structure of society itself was being changed: the old hierarchical society based upon landholding was being challenged by new forces which were threatening to destroy it. The industrial developments of the 1780s and to a lesser extent the agrarian changes of the same years created a new series of relationships which were ultimately to make 'classes' rather than 'interests' the dominant divisions within society. The terminology of the eighteenth-century writers on society had not included class terms since in a hierarchical society (and one upheld moreover by what were believed to be divine sanctions) its members were ranged in orders, interests, ranks. Bishop Butler put the old view in almost classic terms in a sermon to the London Corporation in 1740: 'He who has distributed men into these different ranks ... has formally put the poor under the superintendancy and patronage of the rich. The rich then, are charged by natural providence, as much as by revealed appointment, with the care of the poor.'[6]

This was essentially a static view of society. From the end of the eighteenth century it became increasingly unrealistic to maintain that the internal divisions of society subsisted vertically, in a pattern of mutually dependent interests, whether landed, commercial, industrial or learned. Rather society was coming to consist of individuals, 'the atomized labour-units of an industrial world', as R. J. White calls them, whose loyalties lay with, and whose interests were best represented by, the class to which they belonged – a horizontal dividing up of society, in fact.[7] 'The poor', 'the lower orders', as they had been known hitherto, have become the labouring or working classes, and the connotation this carries of conflict rather than dependence is in itself significant. In political terms these changes spell the death of 'virtual representation' and the coming of the demand for parliamentary reform and ultimately for universal suffrage. But all this was of course still far ahead. A new terminology to express this class-consciousness was not even yet clearly settled: 'in the imperfectly integrated England of the Napoleonic Wars old and new terms and theories existed side by side'.[8]

For the traditional structure of society was resilient. Indeed during this period it was in many ways strengthened by these new forces. The professions, for example, did not yet present any challenge to the old order of society but rather 'for the moment their influence was exerted to strengthen not to weaken it'.[9] The threat of French invasion and the fear of internal revolution strengthened the bonds of deference as the new industrialists 'looked to traditional authority as the only reliable guardians of order and property in a sea of unrest'.[10] Moreover the tradition of habitual respect which the landed classes, and in particular the aristocracy, expected to receive from their local community was not to be lost overnight. The principle of inherited authority, and the patronage and benevolence which went with it, were so deeply ingrained, in the English countryside at least, that the old rulers were carried forward simply by their own momentum, and by that self-assurance in the rightness of their social position and social responsibility which has always been the mark of the English landowner. When the seventh Duke of Bedford put up over five hundred cottages in 1849 at uneconomic rents on his Devon and Bedford estates his agent said that such building 'satisfies an obligation appertaining to the possession of large Estates, and tends to rescue the good will of the peasantry, and it sets an example to other landlords the following of which could not fail to be greatly beneficial'.[11]

If the aristocracy were still conscious of themselves as the leaders of society the squires and the farmers were generally only too willing to accept them in this role. The hunting-field was the supreme place for the display of this leadership, and with it for the development of that partnership between aristocracy and gentry so long a familiar feature within the county. The great hunting passion as it developed during this period well illustrates the hold of the hierarchical society with all its traditions. 'When the pleasures of the chase can be made the means of calling the gentlemen of the country together,' wrote Sir Christopher Sykes in 1792, 'they become really useful and beneficial to society. They give opportunities of wearing off shynesses, dispelling temporary differences, forming new friendships and cementing old, and draw the gentlemen of the country into one closer bond of society.' As hunting grew more and more fashionable in the first third of the nineteenth century, so it developed an etiquette and a mystique of its own, and since this at the same time increased its expense, the major part of which was carried by the aristocracy, this again helped to cement their local leadership.[12] Thompson in fact goes so far as to say that the hunting interest 'was perhaps the most real and fundamentally influential element in county society. As loyalties founded on emotions outrun the calculus of economic interests, so the fox did more for the unity and strength of the landed interest than rent rolls.' It was a brotherhood which excluded the labourer, but apart from him it embraced men from every station of life, bound together by common memories of the excitement and frustration of the chase.

The tenacity of this sort of world is a forcible reminder of the ambivalent character of these years. The growth of a public opinion nurtured on meetings and periodicals, the use of committees, the beginnings of statistical investigation, the development of more sophisticated forms of administration, hint at a new ordering of society, but one which was still far from being realized. This is still the informal world of personality, not yet the impersonal world of institutions. The Webbs looked at these years and saw a decaying and outmoded machinery, obsolete and calling loudly for reform. For them there was little to praise in the last years of the old forms of local government. But they forgot, if indeed they ever fully allowed themselves to recognize, that it was the men and not the institutions who mattered, and the theoretically outmoded organs of county government still in fact represented the vigour and usefulness of county society.

There were two important changes in the structure of the Bench during these years, both a reflection of these general developments within society. The greater participation of the members of the aristocracy in local government is typical both of their continued hold on the local leadership and of their increasing concern about their estates and the local community in general. The greater part played by the clergy at Quarter Sessions is part of that growing professionalization of society and of the wide growth of a humanitarian and reforming concern. The presence of the aristocracy at Quarter Sessions need be mentioned only briefly here, as their central role of Lord Lieutenant and the part they played during the years of internal disturbance will be dealt with more fully later on. But whereas before this date it was unusual to find members of the peerage attending Quarter Sessions regularly, from the end of the eighteenth century they begin to come forward to take their place in local government, some of them as chairmen of the Bench, some as active instigators of reform.[13]

In 1811 Cobbett declared in his *Political Register* that 'In the country more than two-thirds, I believe, of those who attend at the Sessions are clergymen of the Church of England.'[14] By 1833 Hume, speaking in Parliament, put the proportion as high as a half, though the Webbs seem more likely to be accurate in their total of 1,354 in 1832, or one quarter of the whole body.[15] The number of clergy who became Justices during these years makes a striking contrast to the paucity or often complete absence of clerical Justices in the earlier eighteenth century. By the end of it the Cambridgeshire Bench was almost entirely clerical;[16] elsewhere the clergy were the most active and regular members of Quarter Sessions, and there are several examples of sessions at which they outnumbered the lay Justices. In Hereford, Cornwall, Lincoln, Somerset and Norfolk the clergy made up more than half the acting Justices, and therefore it may be assumed, since they generally showed a greater assiduity in their duties, that they must generally have been in the majority.[17] Time and time again it was a clerical Justice who took the lead among his fellow magistrates as chairman of Quarter Sessions, delivering the charge to the Grand Jury and guiding the Court through all the intricacies of criminal law, questioning witnesses, determining legal procedure and giving sentence. The clergy were often renowned for their grasp of law, and certainly one of the law books produced by their number became the classic *par excellence* on any magistrate's shelves: *The Justice of the Peace and Parish Officer* by the Rev. Richard Burn, 1709–85, vicar of Orton in Westmorland, and one of the most active Justices of his county. Miss McClatchey, who has studied the clergy of Oxfordshire during this period, confirms the impression of their ability and energy, and has concluded that up to the 1830s a greater proportion of criminal convictions was undertaken by clerical Justices than by lay, and that in general they stand out as conscientious and hard-working.[18]

Such numbers of clerical magistrates, in a position to influence their fellow Justices both by their presence on the Bench and by the streams of pamphlets which flowed from their pens with such ease and rapidity, naturally played an important part in shaping the activity and interests of Quarter Sessions at this time. The widespread urge for 'improvement' found its natural disciples and promoters among the clerical Justices. Some of their concerns must seem to subsequent ages less praiseworthy than others. They were the leaders, for example, in that crusade 'for the Reformation of the Manners of the Lower Orders' which swept the county Benches between 1786 and 1800. The Rev. Henry Zouch, chairman of the West Riding Quarter Sessions, shows this reforming zeal at its most extreme and unlovely. 'It is found by long experience,' he said, 'that when the common people are drawn together upon any public occasion, a variety of mischiefs are certain to ensue; allured by unlawful pastimes, or even by vulgar amusements only, they wantonly waste their time and money to their own great loss and that of their employers.'[19] Accordingly he made every effort to discourage or prevent all kinds of amusements and even meetings of the poor that might be considered by their local superiors a danger to their morals.

Zouch was also actively concerned with the movement for the reform of prisons – he was responsible for the complete reorganization of the county gaol at Wakefield – and in this he is much more characteristic of the best type of clerical Justice: energetic, constructive, recognizing a crying social evil when others were blind to it, and tireless in organizing his Bench and his locality into action to correct it. In 1764, at a time when no Justice or Sheriff would have dreamt of inspecting the fever-ridden prisons, and ten years even before John Howard's momentous visit to the Bedford gaol, the Rev. George Botts, a Suffolk Justice, was inducing his fellow magistrates to improve the state of a local house of correction.[20] When the reform of its prisons was being discussed between 1760 and 1780 by the Wiltshire Quarter Sessions the names of the Rev. C. Wake and the Rev. J. Rolt appear regularly at the head of the commission in the minute book.[21] The Rev. Samuel Glasse spent a great part of his life inducing the Middlesex magistrates to introduce classification and employment into their prisons.

It was a prebendary of Winchester, the Rev. Edmund Poulter, who was responsible for that well-intentioned, though as it turned out, disastrous experiment, launched by the Berkshire magistrates' meeting at Speenhamland in 1795. Pauperism, that ever-recurring spectre of the magistrate, made worse by the industrial and agrarian changes, became even more acute during the dislocations caused by the French Wars. In 1795 the Berkshire magistrates, inspired by the best motives and anxious to save the semi-starved populace from the terrible conditions of the workhouse, decided upon a system of outdoor relief, ordering the local overseers to supplement wages whenever the price of bread rose beyond a certain amount. They settled a scale, varying according to the number in the family and the price of wheat, which although it applied immediately only to Berkshire, was in fact quickly taken up and soon became general throughout the country. It seemed at first sight an attractive and apparently humane solution to an immense problem, but in fact it amounted to the subsidizing of agricultural wages out of the poor rates and it encouraged all sorts of attendant evils. Before long it was apparent that it was actually promoting pauperism. Farmers kept wages low and independent labourers were forced to accept relief, and thus almost inevitably it placed a bounty on idleness since even the laziest man knew his parish would never let him and his family starve. By 1833 it had become apparent just how far the scheme had failed. The wretched state of the agricultural labourer still remained the foremost social problem, while £7m. had been spent in poor rates in order to achieve little more than the creation of nation-wide pauperism.

As pauperism grew so did crime, for the two were closely allied. In Warwickshire in 1773 there were only three convictions for larceny, theft or fraud in the county; in 1837 there were 445. From 1775 to 1788 there was an average of eight convictions annually; from 1823 to 1832 this had risen to 245·7. In 1775 there were forty-one prisoners in the county gaol; in 1835 there were 351.[22] The reaction to this rising wave of crime was to increase the severity of the penalties. The harshness of the criminal law at this time is startling. In 1819 Sir Thomas Fowell Buxton put the number of capital offences at 223, the great majority of which had been classified as such during the eighteenth century. The crudity, and in many cases the irrationality, of the criminal law, was mitigated in fact by a liberal procedure which encouraged lenient interpretation. Thus since a simple theft of goods above 12d. was considered grand larceny and was punishable with death, the theft would often be valued at under this sum to allow the prisoner to escape the full penalty. Some figures from the Home Circuit for 1785 reveal something of the mind of the Judges: of the sixty-four executions which took place in that year sixty-three were offences against property.[23] At Quarter Sessions the same attitude prevailed: property must be protected at all costs. The increasing severity of the Game Laws shows this particularly well. The enactment of much legislation protecting game was the corollary of the new seriousness towards the pleasures of shooting, by which the old informality gave way to game books and gamekeepers, the strict preservation of game and then its formally organized slaughter. The labouring classes who regarded game as a fair prize for all who could get it, particularly when other food was short, saw nothing wrong in poaching and were naturally antagonized by Game Laws which could decree transportation for those caught poaching at night. The concentration of large numbers of birds in recognized preserves was of course an active inducement to poach, but it was also generally agreed that many agricultural labourers were actually driven to poaching by their acute distress after 1815. Poaching offences in such counties as Bedford or Dorset, where wages were low and unemployment considerable, were high in such years of agricultural distress as 1821–3, and tended to fall away in years of comparative prosperity like 1825–6.[24] A list of fines imposed at Quarter Sessions during these years would almost lead one to think that the endeavours of the country gentry were simply aimed at preserving the interests of the landowners from the predatory habits of the starving poor.

But if the Benches failed signally to tackle the roots of these closely allied problems of pauperism and crime they did at least during these years show themselves enlightened in the care and treatment of the criminals whom they found committed to their charge. The state of the prisons had been a scandal which might have gone unregarded for ever had not John Howard, when pricked as the High Sheriff of Bedfordshire in 1773, obeyed the letter of the law and, as royal representative in the shire, inspected the gaol. What he found there so horrified him that he turned to the local Justices to demand their intervention to stop some at least of the more flagrant abuses. Since they refused to act without a precedent, Howard set out to find one, and thus embarked upon a life of travel and writing in the cause of prison reform. His *State of the Prisons*, published in 1777, stated what he found with brutal starkness. 'I set down matters of fact without amplification,' he wrote. The remedy he left to others: he himself was content to stir the public conscience and to present local government with what was probably the biggest indictment in its history.

How the Benches responded may be seen most clearly by looking in detail at one of the more enterprising and energetic counties, Gloucestershire. Here Howard found that the old castle down by the river which served the county as a gaol was in an appalling condition: hardened criminals mingled with those confined merely on suspicion, there was no separation of men and women, everyone alike was herded in one room so unsafe that at night they had to be secured with irons to one great central chain to prevent their escape. No provision was made for the sick; gaol-fever, a particularly malignant form of typhus, was common. It was doubtless in 1780, the year in which he served as High Sheriff of the county, that Sir George Onesiphorus Paul followed Howard's example and saw these conditions for himself. He then determined to stir the county into activity, but he waited until 1783, when as chairman of the Grand Jury he could address a large and influential section of the community, to make his first public statement. Typical of the well-informed magistrate at his best his speech showed that he had studied the leading European and English authorities on the subject from Beccaria to Blackstone, and was familiar with all the relevant statutes. The task he set before himself and the county showed his determination to go to the heart of the matter. His first step was to attack the indiscriminate confinement of prisoners and to substitute division according to the nature of their crimes. He strongly advocated solitary confinement and hard labour, hoping by a judicious combination of the two to reform as well as to punish.[25] For the next thirty years Paul used every means at his disposal to bring these principles to the attention of his fellow magistrates and the county in general. He wrote pamphlets and addressed public meetings; he prepared resolutions for the Justices and presentations for the Grand Jury; he organized the passing of a local Act, and personally guided the building of the new prison itself which was to embody these ideas in bricks and mortar. And even the undoubted success of the prison itself, opened in

1791, did not satisfy him. From the first he had shown a breadth of outlook which again was typical of the best among the reformers. He believed, as he put it in his pompous manner, that 'the meritorious exertions of individual counties' should lead on to 'a statute of general and decisive obligation'. Accordingly, eight years later the proposals for Gloucestershire were embodied in a general Act applicable to the whole country, and his elaborate *Rules, Orders and Regulations for the Controul and Government of Prisons*, in its four successive editions, ensured that his system could be followed in all its details by other Benches elsewhere.

In the other rudimentary public services provided by local government there was during this period no comparable advance, except that many counties were building themselves handsome Shirehalls as a monument to county government. Quarter Sessions continued to supervise the maintenance of highways and bridges, but while there was still little progress in the appointment of technically qualified surveyors[26] no great advance could be expected in this quarter.

As social problems grew more complex the central government, while still leaving to the counties the day-to-day handling of them, found itself needing more and more information about the state of the countryside and about current social and economic developments. As a result it began to ask Quarter Sessions for accurate statistical information on matters of all kinds. Returns of this nature were not new but they were now demanded with much greater frequency. In 1777 the Benches sent up information on the state of the poor; in 1786 a survey of the charitable donations in the county; in 1776, 1785 and 1803 figures of Poor Law expenditure; in 1781 figures of payments of bounties to flax growers for the Board of Trade; in 1795 lists of the names and places of meeting of Friendly Societies, together with details of their rules and organization; and in 1801 came the first census. Particularly enterprising was the investigation undertaken in 1795 for which the magistrates were to deliver to the Home Office an account of the produce of that year's grain, after a particularly disastrous harvest, compared with the produce of a fair crop in an average year. This involved the Justice in organizing a succession of local meetings with the farmers and clergy in every village. The farmers, unused to such demands, were apprehensive of what this might mean, and in some cases the Justices did not have an easy task. Often however they were able to pass on the burden of collecting information either to the Clerk of the Peace or to the high constables, and since this in many instances involved a fee it was not at all unpopular.

Such demands, by whoever they were ultimately carried out, naturally involved the county administration in much extra work. The burden of business laid upon Quarter Sessions had been growing steadily since Tudor times, but the scope and the direction of the Justices' responsibilities were now being increased in a manner completely without precedent. The social changes of these years would in themselves have presented sufficiently acute problems for any local community to solve without the additional complication of the country being at war from 1793 to 1815. The mobilization of the militia began late in 1792, even before the declaration of the war with France. In 1794 the counties were invited to raise voluntary subscriptions for home defence, particularly units of county cavalry, and by 1796 the government was embarking upon an ambitious programme to treble its size by a supplementary militia.[27] Some of the routine work, such as sending an annual report of militia officers, could be left to the Clerk of the Peace and the ultimate responsibility lay with the Lord Lieutenant, but the main brunt fell upon the deputy lieutenants, most of them also Justices, who had to attempt the thankless task of trying to organize and equip the local yokels into something approaching a useful company. Service in peacetime was among the attractions of county social life: much of the twenty-eight days spent under canvas was passed most agreeably in balls, dinners and hunting. 'We have at present the Players & Puppett Shows, & almost every Night a Rout,' as one Gloucestershire Justice and deputy lieutenant reported to his sister in 1760.[28] But in war-time the talk was all of equipment, training, promotion. The original numbers in most counties were now very considerably swelled by the supplementary militia, and by the volunteer companies, many of them yeomanry cavalry units, which were mushrooming forth in many small towns and villages. Their zeal and loyalty were assured: they felt themselves confident, as a broadside issued from Stow-on-the-Wold put it, of raising a troop 'who may be duly enrolled and disciplined, so as to repel any outrageous insult offered to the Laws and Constitution of this realm'.[19]

The actual work of harnessing this zeal usefully fell to the local landowner. Since each company drew up its own rules, furnished its uniform and settled the terms upon which it was prepared to serve, this meant that he found himself deciding upon its regulations, training and exercising the men, and not infrequently bearing a large proportion of the expense. These regulations, as a result, often reflect their patriarchical authorship. Nathaniel Winchcombe at Frampton-on-Severn, the Gloucestershire clothier Justice, ordered 'every member appearing in his uniform must be perfectly *clean*, his hair combed and propertly cut, his shoes blacked, and every part of his dress decent and in order'. He asked the officers to 'pledge to their honour that they will behave as Gentlemen to every members of the corps', and levied fines on any man cursing or swearing, seen drunk in uniform or 'laughing, talking or being wilfully inattentive when on duty'.[30] One company stated its purposes with a blunt honesty – a determination to serve their King and country with the least possible prejudice to their private concerns. This certainly limited their usefulness. A body of cavalry enrolled in the cloth-manufacturing district of Gloucestershire said they were prepared to serve within the three local hundreds but no farther, 'as the subscribers by far the greater part, are personally extensively engaged in professional or commercial concerns from which they cannot long absent themselves without *incalculable* loss and inconvenience'.[31] These companies saw their role in war-time England, as one of them expressed it, 'to form a respectable body of Housekeepers to aid and assist the Magistrates', in case they should find themselves unsupported 'and the lives and property of the well disposed unprotected'.[32]

For the uncertainties of war only increased the tendencies to disturbance at home, and it was this underlying threat which perhaps more than anything else added to the strain of bearing the office of Justice during these years. For, from 1792 until 1815 and beyond, local government carried out both its routine and its emergency duties in an atmosphere of extreme alarm. The full impact of the fear of revolution was first felt in 1792, a very different thing from the fear of local disorders common enough throughout the eighteenth century. The violence of the revolution in France, the growth of radical agitation at home and the threat that the two might be connected, led the government to take action in issuing a proclamation against seditious writings and to launch a programme of general repression. It was a policy with which the Justices were wholly in accord for, as Lord Grenville, then temporarily in charge of the Home Office, said, the landed gentry were 'thoroughly frightened'.[33] Many Justices joined the 'Association for Preserving Liberty and Property against Republicans and Levellers' which, by means of meetings throughout the country, hunted down sedition and distributed propaganda of a loyalist nature. Already by 1793 it seemed that the forces of radicalism were weakening, and the associations therefore generally began to dissolve themselves. A minority transformed themselves bodily into volunteer corps since it seemed that the chief danger had now become one of invasion. But moral force and military force continued to be employed together, and the local governors felt assured that victory depended upon their maintenance of both. The war thus strengthened the movement for the reform of manners and the enforcement of a stricter morality. Chairmen of the Bench took every possible opportunity of haranguing a captive audience on the first day of Quarter Sessions upon the vital necessity of encouraging the lower orders of society to be more honest, more frugal and more respectable. Amazingly, they were not without success: nearly all contemporary observers commented upon the force of this new morality at every level of society.

War-time therefore added very considerably both to the burden of Quarter Sessions and to the demands made upon the individual Justice out of sessions. Taken all in all it is hardly surprising that whereas in 1787 the Wiltshire Bench found it took them three days to deal with their business, by Trinity 1817 they were sitting for six days, and by Hilary 1819 for eight.[34] Finances corroborate this: in 1792 the county expenditure in Cumberland had been £1,600, in 1830 it had grown to £13,000. In 1786 the

West Riding was spending £7,279 annually, in 1826 £47,787.[35] In 1782 Warwickshire spent £1,803, in 1837 £20,393.[36] The important thing to appreciate however about such growth is that it could not mean merely a straightforward increase of time or expenditure in the traditional ways, but almost inevitably involved the Benches in a search for new methods of dealing with their business. The greater number of days spent sitting as a court encouraged the streamlining and speeding up of procedure, and when a county undertook a large programme of reform, especially of its prisons, this imposed such a strain upon the whole machinery of local government that it almost always led to a more sophisticated handling of local finances, a greater use of salaried officials, a more regular distribution of business among committees. The appointment of a regular chairman of Quarter Sessions from the 1780s was a general move in the direction of a greater stability in court procedure. So much business was delegated to committees during the eighteenth century that standing committees for all aspects of county business became common in the early years of the nineteenth. But perhaps the most significant innovation of all was that now the Benches turned to professionals to help them with their routine duties.

Permanent and salaried officials were not unknown of course in local government for the local Justices had for long relied upon the clerical and administrative help of the deputy clerk of the peace. The Clerk of the Peace himself, an appointment in the hands of the *custos rotulorum*, was generally a gentleman or a man of means who appointed a local attorney in his place. Often the office became a dynastic possession, passed from father to son for several generations. The position was popular because it carried fees, which were in many counties checked and reassessed at intervals by Quarter Sessions, although it was not until 1817 that they were in fact empowered by statute to establish a table of fees.[37] Much of the routine work of arranging the court itself fell to him: drawing up indictments, arraigning prisoners, making out warrants and orders, keeping the jurors' names and recording the judgment of the Bench. The deputy clerk of the peace was also the keeper of the records and the publicity agent of the court, responsible for making the decisions of the court known to the

officials concerned, which might mean printing and circulating
several hundred copies of instructions to high and petty constables
after any important order had been passed by Quarter Sessions.

The office of treasurer was instituted in most counties in the
early years of the eighteenth century, but it was at first rather
casual and haphazard in character. In some counties there was a
separate treasurer for each fund, for bridges, charities, turnpikes
and so on; in others there was a separate treasurer for every
major division of the county. On the whole these men were not
Justices (or if they were they appointed a deputy) but minor
gentry and substantial tradesmen. There was no regular system
of remuneration until they began to receive salaries at the end of
the eighteenth century, and even then these were almost derisory:
until 1809 the treasurer for Gloucestershire received twelve
guineas annually, with an extra five guineas for making out and
printing an abstract of his accounts; in Lancashire in 1798 the
treasurer was receiving £20 although the current balance reached
nearly £4,000; only from about 1815 or 1820 did these get raised
to £200 or £300, though Gloucestershire was still paying £120
in 1824 and Berkshire £150 in 1822. Such salaries seem pitifully
inadequate when the complexity of the finances these men were
expected to handle is considered. Little advance could be made
in organizing a county's money while the Bench still clung to the
old idea that the cost of any particular service should be charged
to whatever section of the community benefited from it, and payment made as the bills fell due. But as the total county expenditure
grew so the inadequacies of such procedure became more and
more apparent. The support of the militiamen's families during
the Napoleonic wars added greatly to the already heavy burdens on
the ratepayer, and when Parliament came to investigate matters in
1830 some counties, such as Sussex, were paying rates of 6s. 9d.
But already by the 1780s many treasurers had begun to lay the
foundations of a county debt. It was often when, in connexion
with a programme of prison building, the counties realized the
inconveniences of meeting capital expenditure out of current
income, that the Justices decided to spread the load by taking up
a loan of £2,000. In subsequent years similar loans might be
made for this or for larger sums. In Wiltshire the securities found

takers from every section of the county with money to invest, from the local gentry to a baker and a blacksmith. In time the county found itself with money to spare and became in turn a lender. By the 1830s the treasurer of Wiltshire was a busy man, handling a turnover sometimes approaching £30,000 and managing both the debts and credits of his county.[38]

That other salaried officer, the county surveyor, was even slower to appear. Though the county was being forcibly reminded in the matter of prisons of its responsibilities for such rudimentary public services it was only with the greatest reluctance that the Justices were willing to admit the necessity of a permanent and professional skilled architect or engineer in the place of their old habit of farming out jobs as they came up to some small bricklayer or carpenter. Even when a county did appoint a surveyor it often seems to have discontinued the office after a number of years. Hampshire in 1777 paid their surveyor a few guineas a time for whatever work he did but then dismissed him in 1784, 'this court having adjudged such office to be unnecessary'. Buckinghamshire had a salaried surveyor of bridges from 1804 to 1822, but then appointed no successor until 1838. Perhaps underlying this was the feeling that any country gentleman who possessed sufficient knowledge of the techniques of building, drainage and engineering to run his estates could by the same token take adequate care of his locality. Certainly, as late as 1825, the Gloucestershire Quarter Sessions tacitly acknowledged the superior knowledge of the local magistrate, for when Collingwood, the county surveyor, reported that a new bridge was needed, they ordered that 'the building of the said bridge be placed under the direction and superintendence of the Rev. Charles Jefferson, whose orders the county surveyor shall obey'.[39] A noteworthy exception to the rule was Shropshire, which appointed Thomas Telford as county surveyor about 1787.

The growing use of these new officials carried with it a most important assumption about the nature of the business carried out at Quarter Sessions. While the old principle of the universal obligation of any community to fulfil its duties still held sway there could be no progress towards any direct administration by the court. For all the old cumbrous machinery of judicial process, presentation, indictment, conviction and fine had to be gone through with all its attendant delays and waste of time and energy. Although by the early nineteenth century the hundred jury and the petty jury had both fallen into disuse, a presentment by the grand jury, made up of substantial farmers and yeomen, was still theoretically necessary before Quarter Sessions could undertake the repair of roads, bridges or any county buildings. This practice was being reduced by now to a formality: presentments were generally prepared beforehand by the Clerk of the Peace or the surveyor, and the process of direct administration was slowly creeping in.[40] The growth of a county executive, however rudimentary, was encouraged by the fact that the court began to make a distinction between its judicial and its administrative business. The latter would be dealt with first, in some private room either at the Shirehall or some local inn, before the Justices moved in a body to hold open court in the prescribed manner. In this there was nothing sinister, as the Webbs believed, and far from conducting their business in secret the magistrates always welcomed the presence of the press. The rules of procedure, drawing together the haphazard reforms of the past fifty years, which were being published in most counties in the early years of the nineteenth century, are some indication of a movement towards a greater efficiency and regularity which had been achieved in an unspectacular manner in response to the new demands laid upon local government.

To talk in terms of a new bureaucracy is misleading: English government was not yet a matter of institutions – it was still a world of personality and of personal contact. Samuel Bamford received a tremendous shock when actually brought face to face with England's governors and taken before the Privy Council for interrogation in 1817. 'Quite a merry set of gentlemen', he found them, and he went away feeling that this kind of meeting ought to happen more often. But then he was a working-class man and to him 'the government' had probably been little more than an abstraction. To the more politically active members of society it was more familiar. The Lord Lieutenants naturally enough spent a considerable part of their time in London, except when emergencies required their residence in their native county. The local M.P.s, who more often than not were also members of their local Benches, were frequently at Westminster and familiar with the pattern of the day-to-day working of government. Other local gentry and attorneys also saw something of the government at work when they came up to give evidence at the bar of the House of Commons in connexion with the promotion of some local Act. It was quite usual for witnesses to have to spend a week or two at some London inn waiting to be called, and there were in every county a handful of local attorneys who had made themselves familiar with House of Commons procedure and who could be counted on to serve local interests when any county matter came before the House.[41] For such men therefore the government was not something entirely remote. They would not have been as startled as Bamford to discover that Lord Sidmouth's manner 'was affable and much more encouraging to freedom of speech than I had expected'.[42] They felt that the government was approachable and therefore they did not hesitate to approach it.

The Home Office, with which the Justices dealt most frequently since the Home Secretary was enjoined to keep the King's peace and was therefore concerned for the well-being of society in general, was run on extremely informal lines. It was ridiculously under-staffed: it numbered no more than twenty-nine in 1823. The Home Office papers now deposited in the Public Record Office give a very clear idea of the voluminous correspondence which went through its hands, not merely from the Lord Lieutenants, from whom it naturally expected to receive official communications, but also from local magistrates who do not seem to have hesitated to report their fears of unrest or to relay information which they believed important. All the evidence, in fact points to a closer, and a more informal, relationship between the central and local governments than has generally been assumed. The Webbs, for instance made it one of the central themes of their great work that throughout the eighteenth century the local Benches were working in more or less complete auto-nomy. Dowdell had concluded that 'there was danger in action, but little, if any, in inaction. The Justices worked, so to speak, under negative but not under positive supervision. Here was a powerful incentive to a *laissez-faire* attitude.'[43] Professor J. D.

Chambers indeed has gone so far as to say, 'It [the county] was now left to live its own life, free not only from control from the centre, but even from guidance and supervision.'[44]

Twice a year the Benches were brought into very immediate and direct contact with the central government when the county gathered at the Assizes, an event which was also something of a social occasion: Sidney Smith spoke of York's three weeks of 'dancing and provincial joy'.[45] As in Elizabeth's day the Judges came not only in their strictly judicial capacity to deal with the more serious criminal cases, but more generally as agents of the central government to advise the local Justices and to inform them of any new developments in the government's policy. Before setting out they received detailed instructions about the charge they were to give in their opening speech. Sometimes they drew attention to some specific programme the government was trying to promote, as in 1787 when the reform movement against vice and immorality was launched. Sometimes they insisted on the particularly strict execution of some new piece of legislation. Since it was not until 1797 that the government allowed the circulation of copies of statutes for the use of the magistrates this was most important. The Judges also expected to oversee, and if necessary confirm, any important business conducted at Quarter Sessions since their last visit. The regulations for the new prisons, or the tables of fees for Justices' clerks for example, were laid before them. Their assent was by no means automatic. It is not unusual to find a note scribbled in the margin of a minute book that the Judges had disapproved of certain orders 'and intimated that their Power extended to the confirming and not altering of any Rules, recommended that the same be done and laid before them at the next Assizes'.

This raises a fundamental question: had the government any consistent policy towards the localities, and if so, could it put it into effective operation? At intervals the government is clearly trying to stir the Justices into greater activity, and in between the Assizes Quarter Sessions might receive a circular letter accompanying some new proclamation or Act. These were particularly common in any emergency, such as the severe corn shortage of 1795, or the distress caused by rising prices after 1800.

But almost always such efforts were short-lived: a year later there is silence on the subject, and whether the government is satisfied or not with local activity it lets the matter drop. Its intervention is thus essentially intermittent, spasmodic and uncoordinated, scarcely worthy to be designated policy. Yet it would be wrong to conclude from this that there was not any positive relationship between the two: there was a very real relationship in fact, a partnership in which the localities played an active role. They turned to the central government, particularly of course to the Home Office, for help and advice, but they did not hesitate to criticize government measures when they felt it necessary and to suggest amendments and improvements. The county had its own contributions to make towards solving the most important social questions of the day and local Acts far outnumber general public Acts during this period.[46] Enclosure, the Poor Law, canals, prison reform, the rudimentary beginnings of state welfare in fact, were all matters in which local knowledge ensured workable legislation. The history of prison reform demonstrates how often the general Act passed by the Commons proved a mere blue-print, excellent in intention but unworkable in practice, and real progress in social reform came by way of such an Act as that of 1791, originally applicable to Gloucestershire and then extended to the country as a whole.

The close relations between county and central government were not, however, allowed to become too close. The Duke of Portland had once actually to reprimand a Lord Lieutenant for the frequency of his correspondence and his habit of seeking help upon small matters of uncertainty, for to carry this to an extreme would, he said, threaten to introduce a 'principle which would be very injurious and derogatory to the respectability which now belongs to the Magistracy of the county'.[47] The government was careful to encourage the independence of the localities and promised to stand by their decisions and actions when these were well-intentioned. The classic instance of this came after Peterloo when the magistrates ordered the military to disperse a Manchester crowd gathered to hear Orator Hunt and eleven people were killed in the fighting which ensued. Lord Sidmouth, when he conveyed the thanks of the Prince Regent to the magistrates, was acting on what he believed to be an essential principle of government – to acquire the confidence of the magistracy by readiness to support them 'in all honest, reasonable and well-intentioned acts, without inquiring too minutely whether they might have performed their duty a little better or a little worse'.[48]

Perhaps the best way in which to appreciate the mutual confidence subsisting between Westminster and the localities is to consider those years up to 1819 when it seemed that the smouldering fires of discontent might flare into open revolt and engulf this country in a revolution comparable to that across the Channel. For a brief period, in April and May 1812, twelve thousand troops were being distributed about the disturbed manufacturing districts of England, an army larger than that with which Wellesley set sail for Portugal in 1808. Rumours were circulating that a general armed rising was planned, the authorities were scared, there was talk of a 'direct Road to an open Insurrection'.[49] How near was England to revolution in the early years of the nineteenth century? And if she did in fact escape to what extent was this due to the efficiency with which the Justices put into force the machinery of law and order at their disposal? For the peace-keeping machinery of England during the Napoleonic wars was more or less what it had been during the years of the Armada. The Justice himself remained the essential guardian of established order; only London possessed a small, regular police force; elsewhere the police were voluntary and amateur. The Home Office had no servants or subordinates in the provinces. Secret agents were employed quite arbitrarily on a haphazard basis, amateurs who offered their services and were paid by results – 'no sedition, no pay' was bound to mean that there was in fact no shortage of sedition.[50] Anything beyond this, and this meant obviously a very great deal, depended upon the Justices and the forces they controlled.

Three instruments were available to suppress riots, all of which could be called out by the magistrates. The first, voluntary defence associations, could be instituted by any loyal minority and their expenses paid by voluntary subscriptions. When these failed to materialize resort could be had to a compulsory levy, the old system of watch and ward revised and brought up to date by an Act of 1812. Both these were undertaken only occasionally and spasmodically, and on the whole proved weak and ineffective in action. This left the militia. But often its local character and associations detracted from its usefulness in suppressing riots expressing local grievances. Its members found the putting down of local unrest both unpopular and unpleasant; as one Justice recognized, 'our men thought when they became soldiers of fighting nothing but the French, and therefore did not approve of that very disagreeable service, quelling riots'.[51] In the last resort the magistrates could turn to the military, and they did call in military force surprisingly often. The forces were under the command of their own officers but at the disposal of the civil authorities, and the area commander would only plan his actions after consultation with the magistracy. Portland's letters to the local authorities always assured them that the commanding officer was ordered to follow their directions and the presence of troops was merely to strengthen the civil arm, but at the height of the Luddite rising the industrial areas had taken on a surprisingly military appearance, with soldiers quartered in every inn, and great camps established in Sherwood Forest and on Kersal Moor. Garrisons, military patrols, the coming and going of large bodies of troops, gave great tracts of the north and midlands a warlike air which made a mockery of that gentlemanly assumption on the part of the government that property should protect itself and that if the Justices were sufficiently vigilant they ought to be able to keep the peace as well as their forefathers had done before them.

The English still pinned their faith to the amateur, the unprofessional, even if this meant also the casual and the inadequate. The suggestion of instituting a professional police force, trained, controlled and paid for by local taxation, was greeted with cries of horror as 'continental' and 'tyrannous'.[52] The government and the public in general assumed instead that there were throughout the country local gentry of integrity and ability who could be counted upon to defend the rights of property and restrain society within its proper channels. The government was ready to advise and support, but it left the initiative with the Justices.

In some cases this faith was justified. Among the Home Office papers recur the names of the most active and industrious Justices, above all the ubiquitous Rev. Mr Hay, for nearly twenty years chairman of the Manchester and Salford Bench, one of the most trusted agents of the Home Office, who practically constituted himself police-magistrate for his locality. The Rev. Mr Becher of Southwell and the Rev. Mr Prescott of Stockport were two other particularly vigorous clerics; Mr Sherbrooke was energetic in the Luddite areas of Nottinghamshire, and Sir Joseph Radcliffe near Huddersfield. But these were exceptional men, the men who had the determination and the ability to stir their neighbourhoods into activity. Elsewhere many magistrates, unable to see the wood for the trees, fussed nervously at the least suspicious happenings and wrote anxiously to the Home Secretary about the hatching of most improbable plots and the movements of highly unlikely spies. Many more were apathetic until events forced them to take action, and then that action came so late that it could only mean the calling in of the military.[53]

'The prevailing impression certainly was that there was a want of vigilance and activity in the magistracy,' wrote the Home Secretary to the Nottinghamshire magistrates in 1816.[54] The tone, as R. J. White says, is rather that of the squire addressing a careless gamekeeper. The simile is in many ways illuminating. The concept of government is still the classic and Tory one, embodied in Sidmouth's final sentence: 'Government could do no more than give the impulse and all the aid that could be afforded, to the execution of the laws.' The weakness of this sort of argument at first seems blatant: the very idea of hoping to control the wide and growing insubordination by a handful of local gentry, supported by voluntary well-wishers and yokels roped into the militia, with the regular army in the background, has all the elements of absurdity, such as only a nation wedded to the idea of the amateur could possibly conceive.

And yet everyone in Regency England knew that the structure of power did not depend upon London or the government's military barracks. It still rested upon deference, with its corollary, fear. Just as the county gentry accepted and welcomed aristocratic leadership, and the mutual confidence between them made it possible for local affairs to be carried on smoothly, so did they enjoy the confidence of the men below them. The Justice shared the outlook of the governing classes but he also shared the outlook of the governed. 'There was no isolation about his life. Every day brought him close to the common life of the common people. He was unlikely to be troubled by any such entity as "the mob": he knew too much about Tom and Dick and Harry.'[55] So long as this held true the government showed its wisdom in making use of the national social structure. But this world was passing, and in some places passing quickly. Soon urban life, the press, the growth of public meetings and political discussions, were to challenge and to make a mock of the traditional order of landowner and dependants. Fortunately for England no really serious unrest broke out after 1819, and it was left to the new era, inaugurated by the Reform Bill of 1832, to attempt to resolve that tension between the deference owed to the hierarchical society and the respect due to the new social, economic and political elements which refused any longer to recognize or accept that deference.

Yet strong as they were, the county Justices found themselves under attack during the fifty years from 1780 to 1830 in a way that was unprecedented in their history. It was not on account of their oligarchical nature or their corrupt handling of affairs, as were the protests made against the urban Benches during these years, nor had the county Justices forfeited the general respect and trust of those they governed as the borough magistrates undoubtedly had done by this time.[56] They were certainly not guilty of pursuing their own material ends, and in fact their activity in promoting reforms of prisons, Poor Law and other aspects of county administration had made inroads into their private wealth because of the vastly increased county rate. In one particular however they showed themselves open to a gross, even tyrannical abuse of their authority: their execution of the Game Laws aroused universal indignation. 'There is not a worse constituted tribunal on the face of the earth,' Brougham told the House of Commons in 1828, 'than that at which summary convictions on the Game Laws take place. . . . I mean . . . a brace of sporting magistrates'.[57] No doubt many of the stories that circulated about Game Law prosecutions were embroidered in the telling, but a typical episode is vividly recounted by Sir Spencer Walpole:

In 1822 a farmer coursing hares on his own land, with the permission of his own landlord, was summoned by the keeper of the adjoining landowner for doing so. The adjoining landowner in this particular instance was the Duke of Buckingham, and the farmer was literally convicted by the Duke himself, in the Duke's private house, at the instance of one of the Duke's keepers, and on the evidence of another of his keepers.[58]

If tenants and agricultural labourers felt the sting here, increasing numbers of townsfolk found themselves experiencing the same severity of judicial authority in favour of the sanctity of landed property. In their case it concerned the stopping up of footpaths. After 1815 any two J.P.s together might summarily close any footpath they deemed unnecessary, subject only to appeal at the following Quarter Sessions. This all too easily became an invaluable instrument in the hands of any unscrupulous magistrate who felt like excluding the public from his land, particularly that new urban public which was beginning to encroach on the countryside. When the citizens of the new northern and midland towns found their access to fields closed by an arbitrary stopping up of ancient footpaths Radical members began to protest in the House of Commons about such a shameless robbery of the public.

Discontent with the Justices was not strong enough to demand that they should be abolished in favour of paid stipendiaries. The very idea was anathema to Whig, Tory and Radical alike. 'A set of rural judges,' exclaimed Sidney Smith in disgust, 'in the pay of the government, would very soon become corrupt jobbers and odious tyrants, as they often are on the Continent.'[59] The experiment of appointing twenty-four salaried magistrates to the Middlesex Bench was not repeated elsewhere. A stipendiary magistrate was established for Manchester in 1813, but in 1814 the Home Secretary refused to support Brighton in a similar proposal, and no more were created. Stipendiaries would be professionals, they would be expensive, they would be agents of the central government – this was enough to damn them in the eyes of the general public and to leave the way open for the continuing regime of the unpaid amateur in the best English tradition.

References

1. *Portrait of an Age*, Oxford University Press, 2nd edn, 1953, p. 4.
2. D. Spring, 'The Clapham Sect: Some Social and Political Aspects', *Victorian Studies*, 1961, v, No. 1, p. 39.
3. Quoted D. Spring, 'Victorian Aristocracy', *Victorian Studies*, 1963, vi, No. 3, p. 279.
4. This is discussed more fully in 'Victorian Aristocracy'.
5. *ibid.*, p. 279.
6. Quoted Asa Briggs, 'Middle-class consciousness in English politics 1780–1846', *Past and Present*, 1956, ix, p. 65.
7. R. J. White, *Waterloo to Peterloo*, Heinemann, 1957, p. 71 (Penguin Books, 1968).
8. Briggs, *op. cit.*, p. 65.
9. R. Robson, *The Attorney in Eighteenth Century England*, Cambridge University Press, 1959, p. 6.
10. F. M. L. Thompson, *English Landed Society in the Nineteenth Century*, Routledge, 1963, p. 185.
11. D. Spring, *The English Landed Estate in the Nineteenth Century: its Administration*, John Hopkins, Baltimore, 1963, p. 52.
12. For a most illuminating discussion of the influence of fox-hunting on society, see Thompson, *op. cit.*, pp. 144–50.
13. S. and B. Webb, *English Prisons under Local Government*, Longmans, 1922, p. 54.
14. 22 May 1811, xix, p. 1,256. Quoted E. Halévy, *A History of the English People in 1815*, Benn, 1924, i, p. 65, note 4.
15. S. and B. Webb, *The Parish and the County*, 1906, p. 384, note 2.
16. Though in this case many were probably connected with the University so that the county cannot be taken as typical. cf. D. Spring, *Landed Estate*, p. 57.
17. It should be noted however that there were certain Lord Lieutenants who made it a rule never to appoint clergy to the magistracy, and that as a result in Kent, Sussex and Derbyshire there were no clerical Justices.
18. D. McClatchey, *Oxfordshire Clergy 1777–1869*, Oxford University Press, 1960, Chapter XII *passim*.
19. Quoted Webbs, *The Parish and the County*, p. 357.
20. *ibid.*, p. 355.
21. W. R. Ward, 'County Government 1660–1835', *V.C.H. Wiltshire*, 1957, v, p. 176.
22. P. Styles, *Development of County Administration in the late XVIIIth and early XIXth centuries, illustrated by the Records of the Warwickshire Court of Quarter Sessions 1773–1837*, 1934, p. 22.

23. L. Radzinowicz, *History of the English Criminal Law*, Stevens, 1948, I, p. 151.
24. See Thompson, *op. cit.*, pp. 136–44.
25. For a fuller discussion of Paul's beliefs, see my article 'Sir George Onesiphorus Paul', *Gloucestershire Studies*, ed. H. P. R. Finberg, Leicester University Press, 1957, pp. 195–225.
26. See page 118 below.
27. For a more technical consideration of this subject, see J. R. Western, *The English Militia in the Eighteenth Century*, Routledge, 1965.
28. Gloucestershire Record Office (after this G.R.O.) D151/131.
29. Home Office Papers, Public Record Office (after this H.O.) 50/339.
30. G.R.O. D149/997.
31. 4 May 1798, Sir George Onesiphorus Paul to Lord Berkeley, H.O. 50/335.
32. 1798 Lechlade. H.O. 50/335.
33. For a fuller discussion of these years, see Austin Mitchell, 'The Association Movement of 1792–3', *Historical Journal*, 1961, IV, No. I, p. 57.
34. Ward, *op. cit.*, p. 180.
35. Webbs, *The Parish and the County*, p. 192, note 1.
36. Styles, *op. cit.*, p. 22.
37. See Return of Fees Payable to the Clerk of the Peace in the Counties, Parliamentary Papers, 1818, xv.
38. Ward, *op. cit.*, pp. 189–94.
39. Webbs, *The Parish and the County*, pp. 515–16, 520–21.
40. An Act of 1768 had allowed sudden repairs up to £30 to be ordered in an emergency by two Justices. In 1812 ordinary repairs up to £20 might be executed without a presentment. Webbs, *ibid.*, p. 451.
41. The committee books for these local Acts have not survived for the House of Commons but it is interesting to see from those of the House of Lords the numbers of local gentry, clergy, attorneys and farmers journeying to London to be examined and to give evidence before the House.
42. Quoted White, *op. cit.*, p. 36.
43. *A Hundred Years of Quarter Sessions: the Government of Middlesex from 1660 to 1760*, Cambridge University Press, 1932, p. 15.
44. *Nottinghamshire in the Eighteenth Century*, 1932, p. 45.
45. *The Letters of Sidney Smith*, ed. Nowell C. Smith, Oxford University Press, 1953, I, p. 377.
46. W. S. Holdsworth, *History of English Law*, 1938, x, p. 189.
47. 1796. H.O. 43/8/305.
48. G. Pellew, *Life of Lord Sidmouth*, London, 1847, III, p. 262.
49. F. O. Darvall, *Popular Disturbances and Public Order in Regency England*, Oxford University Press, 1934, p. 310.
50. White, *op. cit.*, p. 107.
51. 1802. Rev. William Lloyd Baker, Lloyd Baker papers, Hardwicke Court, Gloucestershire.

52. White, *op. cit.*, p. 107.
53. The Home Office papers contain a vast amount of hysterical writing from the local magistrates which now makes highly entertaining reading but must have been most trying for the already overburdened Home Secretary.
54. Pellew, *op. cit.*, p. 152.
55. White, *op. cit.*, p. 41.
56. See pages 178–9 below.
57. Speech in the House of Commons 7 February 1828, quoted Webbs, *The Parish and the County*, p. 599.
58. *History of England*, I, p. 159, quoted Webbs, *ibid.*
59. *Edinburgh Review*, September 1826, quoted Webbs, *ibid.*, p. 606.

CHAPTER SIX

1834–1888
'The Rural House of Lords'

THE Poor Law Reform of 1834 introduced into English local government the fundamentally new principles of paid officials dependent upon a central government department, and an inspectorate carrying out a code of regulations. Two years later a Royal Commission on County Rates proposed County Councils with representatives from the Boards of Guardians sitting side by side with the Justices. The following years, 1837–8, saw the Highways Act Report proposing changes in the county boundaries. All seemed set in those vigorous years following the passing of the Reform Bill for an administrative revolution which would change the familiar face of local government and remove some of its more anachronistic features. Yet it took half a century for any thoroughgoing reform to be achieved. For the greater part of the reign of Victoria, during years which saw unprecedented economic growth, the coming of the railways, the telegraph, the cheap press, the development of public opinion and above all the growing acceptance of representative institutions, the Bench of Justices still continued much as it had done for the previous four centuries: the same type of men still held their Quarter Sessions four times a year, and still clung, despite the creation of many new authorities around them, to the old familiar county ways. Their tenacity of purpose, and their resilience in the face of the changing order of things, is amazing. How and why should the Justices survive so triumphantly in a world which seemed to shout its belief in representative institutions with ever-increasing force and conviction? This question is central to any assessment of the magistracy in the years between the Poor Law Reform Act and the introduction of County Councils in 1888.

'This Bill will totally abrogate all the local government of the

Kingdom,' wrote Cobbett, as always a pessimist and an alarmist, of the new Act in 1834. Horrified protest came not only from the ultra-left but also from the ultra-right. The traditionalist Tory Oastler was if anything more severe in condemning it and in prophesying dire consequences. It was nothing more, he said, than 'a direct attack on the constitution, on the magistracy, on the land, on the rights of private property and on the last remaining hopes of industrious poverty'.[1] The Act of 1834 did indeed make a dramatic break with the past, though not quite in the terms in which Cobbett or Oastler saw it. The voluminous minutes of evidence of the assistant commissioners reporting in detail upon specific areas, the recommendations of the Commissioners, and above all the text of the Report itself, widely distributed in popular octavo form, brought to the whole question of poor relief the widest possible publicity.

Judged by modern standards the Report has many shortcomings, not least its neglect of the problem of industrial unemployment, but for contemporaries it put the treatment of poverty into a manageable, practical form and into a new intellectual light. It attacked the allowance system created by the Speenhamland scheme in 1795 and now shown up in all its deficiencies as the creator of widespread and ever-increasing pauperism. It strongly asserted that the productive efficiency of the worker which was being virtually destroyed under the old Poor Law must be restored, and recommended a strict administration of relief, so that the conditions of receiving it should exclude the independent labourer. This was known as the principle of 'less eligibility'. From this principle developed almost inevitably the 'workhouse test' for the able-bodied, that is to say, the refusal of any relief outside the workhouse. The sick, the aged and the indigent would of course still be looked after under the Poor Law: indeed it was hoped that they would now be treated better than before since those not truly deserving of relief were to be removed from its sphere.[2] Parishes were to be grouped in unions controlled by Boards of Guardians who were to be elected on a rate-paying franchise (with plural voting according to the amount of rates paid) and held responsible for keeping proper records and accounts. Resident Justices of the

Peace became *ex officio* Guardians. These local authorities were to be supervised by the 'Triumvirate', as they were soon to be known, a commission of three, who were given wide powers of issuing orders and making rules and regulations with the force of law. None of the Commission members were allowed to sit in Parliament, and they were thus free of ministerial control though required to submit an annual report of their proceedings to the Secretary of State.

Such an arrangement brought to an end the rule, actual or possible, of 15,500 uncontrolled petty tyrants dominating their parishes. Contemporaries however were alarmed – not only were the principles embodied in the Act unpopular but the means of its execution appeared threatening and sinister: the heavy hand of Whitehall reaching out to all corners of the land, an attack upon the liberties and freedom of English local government. The Commissioners, it is true, managed within the first two or three years to organize most of the country into unions, and they had begun fairly successfully to apply the workhouse test to the south. But when in 1836 they turned their attention to the midlands and north they met with fierce opposition, strengthened by an economic crisis which hit trade and industry and caused widespread unemployment which was to last until the early 1840s.

In the north the movement for legislation to shorten working hours joined forces with those fighting the introduction of the new Poor Law, and the Commissioners found an even more formidable opposition. The patriarchal Toryism of Richard Oastler, the fiery eloquence of J. R. Stephens and later of Feargus O'Connor, together with the support of many Tory Justices, not only attempted to make the Act unenforceable in the north but demanded its repeal for the country as a whole. The countryside rang with tales of dramatic episodes. At Todmorden John Fielden summoned his factory hands by mill-bell when the emissaries of the Commissioners entered the bounds of the parish, and the police were stripped naked and driven out. The troops had to be called out in Bradford, while in Huddersfield the intimidation was so continuous and so successful that for two years the union could not work effectively. Only the beginnings of

Chartism distracted attention from the immediate opposition and absorbed it into a wider movement of protest.

The Poor Law question brought to light most of the different attitudes which were to recur throughout the middle years of the nineteenth century whenever the government attempted any sequel to this first step of its administrative revolution. These are worth considering in a certain amount of detail since the battle over centralization is of the greatest importance in the development of local government during this period.

A large part of the countryside, with the magistracy frequently its strongest spokesmen, thought still in terms of a traditional pattern of duty. The ideal of the well-regulated village dominated and cared for both in body and mind by a patriarchal parson and squire died hard – and indeed in many places was still as vigorous as it had ever been. Many of the new industrial workers flocking to the towns had in fact been brought up in villages where such conditions prevailed and they were therefore only too happy to accept the benevolence meted out by paternalistic mill-owners in the tradition of Oastler. For many of the mill-owners themselves the goal of a successful business life was the acquisition of a country property together with all the privileges and the responsibilities which went with the ownership of land. But patriarchal attitudes, however well-intentioned, could never go to the roots of the problems of an industrial society and the shortcomings as well as the successes of the mills run on feudal principles are all too clearly illustrated time and again in the succession of reports of the Factory Commissioners. The coal-mine at Flockton was typical: all the concern of the owners and the ladies of the manor for the welfare of the workers in providing Sunday schools, recreation clubs and a sports ground, could not absolve them from allowing their workers to continue in conditions in the pits which as small owners they could not improve but which were by all accounts appalling.[3]

Local feeling, not far removed from this sort of paternalism, was still a force to be reckoned with in the nineteenth century, despite such new factors unifying the country as the railways, telegraph and press. Regional and local diversity were still strong, as Hippolyte Taine recognized when he decided, on a stay in this country in 1859, to visit as many places as possible outside London. 'One ought to try and see the local districts, for it is not possible to understand the social fabric properly until one has studied three or four of its component threads in detail.' [4] Provincial pride of the best sort and glorying in one's native countryside in the tradition of the Elizabethan antiquarians soon shaded off, however, into the much less attractive desire to protect local vested interests from the prying eye, and even more, the active intervention, of the central government. One of the most extreme cases of this kind of short-sighted action was that of Brighton under its M.P., Captain Pechell, who fought centralization in every shape and form until he had so far succeeded in keeping the city free from the clutches of Whitehall that in 1854 Lord Palmerston, admittedly never a man to mince his words, wrote that it was now 'a triumph of prejudice and ignorance and private interest. . . '. [5]

The magistrates, as they watched this invasion of their empire by a central army of paid officials appointed by Whitehall, would however defend their position not in terms of mere self-interest but in terms of an abstract ideal of good government. For it was a widely held belief that too much central government would discourage local self-government and lessen individual self-reliance. This school of thought found support among such widely diverse writers as Charles Kingsley, Coleridge, Hallam and Toulmin Smith. The latter, as a historian, emphasized the Anglo-Saxon elements within the British Constitution, particularly the tradition of self-government which he insisted had, since the time of the folk-moot of Alfred, formed the strongest bulwark of English liberty. Centralization, he declared categorically, in *Centralisation or Representation* published in 1848, and again in *Government by Commissioners, Illegal and Pernicious*, which appeared the following year, was both un-English and unconstitutional. Yet one wonders how seriously such ideas were taken by the educated thinking English public, the magistracy, for example. Was the debate on centralization really related, as Professor Finer suggests, to two broader intellectual movements, to the clash between a 'new brooding Teutonic school' which included the writers mentioned above, and a francophile school of which Bentham, John Mill and Edwin Chadwick formed a part?[6] There was a great contradiction between high-sounding sentiment and concrete action, a contradiction particularly well illustrated by *The Times*, as ever the voice of England. Repeatedly it denounced centralization, yet it supported nearly every measure of social reform passed during the very same years; like the governing class it represented, it did not adhere too firmly to the principles it proclaimed.[7] Toulmin Smith lamented this behaviour: 'We are losing sight daily of principles and allowing ourselves to be made the dupes of presumptuous empiricism.'[8]

Empiricism provides the key to the rate and the extent of administrative growth during this period. For while the Justices could have the satisfaction of unfurling, metaphorically at least, banners with high-sounding legends enunciating the preservation of Anglo-Saxon liberties, they also had the satisfaction of co-operating with the central government in forwarding movements which on the whole they approved. They did in fact largely approve the new Poor Law. In 1836 Charles Mott said 'nearly all men of property and respectability are generally in favour of it', and this was natural enough, as Oastler pointed out, since it favoured the rights of property over the rights of the poor.[9] So that, contrary to first appearances, the history of local government in the nineteenth century continues the tradition of a partnership between Westminster and the localities, a partnership now symbolized by the inspector, whose experience and status, embodying as he did the authority of the central government, were often decisive in local affairs. The years 1833–54 saw much improvement in local government under the tutelage of this new race of men, as larger units of administration were formed, better records were kept and more effective and more humane measures were adopted.

How new were the problems which faced the nineteenth-century Benches? It is all too easy to explain the progress, or rather excuse the lack of it, in nineteenth-century social reform by saying that the government, both central and local, found an entirely novel situation, and had not only to think out solutions from first essentials but also to create *de novo* the machinery by which they were put into force. 'England was in the process of learning how to administer its localities under conditions for which there were no precedents' is the sort of statement which it is all too easy to make.[10] But take four of the major reforms of the 1830s: the appointment of the first factory inspectors in 1833, the establishment of the Poor Law Commissioners in 1834, the beginning of prison inspection in 1835, and the creation of the metropolitan police in 1839. The social evils with which they dealt were none of them new: legislation had been passed in the previous century for three of them and the Factory Act of 1802 had attempted to deal with the fourth.[11] Nor does it seem necessary to say that the administrators sought to put into practice a centralized system of government patterned on a particular theory, or that the nineteenth-century revolution in government must be understood as essentially Benthamite in origin and inspiration.

Perhaps the word 'uniformity' might be more illuminating than the word 'centralization', with all its peculiar overtones. The central government in the nineteenth century was really concerned with creating and imposing uniform standards throughout the country within the framework of local autonomy. The basic principles which defined the growth of the nineteenth-century state were well put by Viscount Howick in connexion with the 1835 Prison Act. The intention of the government, he said, was to leave 'the actual detailed administration to local authorities, but to subject them to the supervision and control of some central authority who should see that the duties were efficiently performed'.[12]

Government was still, by twentieth-century standards, a limited affair. In 1833 the central administration did little more than administer justice, collect taxes and defend the realm. The Home Office, the nerve-centre of internal government, was still staffed by only thirty-nine people. Contemporary opinion held that government should be severely limited; education for example was regarded as the responsibility not of the state but of the individual. It believed also in the excellence of individual philanthropy, and much was still left to voluntary societies and charities even though the 1838 Commission on Charitable Activities revealed their abuses, and pointed out their inadequacy to deal with contemporary social problems. 'Faith in voluntary institutions ran deep in English mentality,' writes an American historian of nineteenth-century Britain.[13] Even more formidable was the Victorian reluctance to interfere with the rights of property, whether land, mines, railways or factories. And contemporaries were of course always horrified at the prospect of any increase in expenditure. Tory indignation was particularly fierce on this point: they regarded the government as already sufficiently large and extravagant. So again, although at the back of their minds this faith in the virtues of local self-government inherited as a going concern from their Anglo-Saxon fore-fathers still persisted, it was overlaid by a belief in non-interference which derived its main force from an attachment to the rights of property, to low taxes and to the preservation of local offices.

Such duties therefore as the legislation of the 1830s imposed upon the Justices were not so much new as an extension of business long familiar to the Bench: prisons and asylums, the poor, the keeping of order, maintaining the highways, all these had been in the Justices' care throughout the previous century. Prisons formed the major part of county expenditure until the establishment of the police force in 1839, and it was to a large extent the mounting costs of maintaining prisoners which brought this branch of the magistrates' work so soon under the eye of the central government. The Select Committee on County Rates emphasized that the increasing costs of prosecuting criminals, transporting prisoners to gaol and financing prison building, were responsible for sending up the county rate so rapidly in the early years of the nineteenth century. After 1835, under the provisions of an Act passed 'for effecting greater uniformity of practice in the government of the several prisons of England and Wales', all local prisons were regularly visited by a Home Office inspector. Separation of different classes of prisoners and improvement of their diet were the central points in the new policy. Yet in spite of all the authority and the experience which the inspectors could bring to bear in local affairs the real reins of power still remained quite firmly in the hands of the local govern-ors. They appointed their own officers, they drew up rules and regulations and above all they controlled expenditure. The magistracy were quite prepared to cooperate with the central inspectors over their irksome duties but they jealously guarded their control over the spending of money raised from the county rate. The authority of the Home Office was limited to sanctioning the rules made by the Justices, and if the reports of the four inspectors on the conduct of the prisons were adverse it could still do no more than deliver a verbal reprimand.[14] It was not until the passing of the Prisons Act of 1865 that the inspectors, in case of conflict with the Justices, could rely on anything more than 'the uncertain weapons of persuasion and publicity, backed by the imponderable authority of a Secretary of State'.[15] This Act so strengthened the control of the central department that all 193 local prisons were forced into the uniform regimen prescribed by the Home Office and the local variations in diet, treatment and discipline which had resisted with such vigour the attempts of the inspectors, were at last ironed out.

Between 1835 and 1862 parish highways were governed by an Act of 1835, which showed surprisingly little advance on the original Elizabethan statute. It did, it is true, bring to an end that ancient obligation laid on every parishioner to render statute duty and team labour, and it enabled the vestry to nominate instead a surveyor with power to levy a rate. The Justices' power of 'presentment' was replaced by an immediate fine to the surveyor himself which finally removed one anomaly of the business of road maintenance. But the surveyors were still amateurs, 'for the most part farmers and others engaged in other pursuits who render their services gratuitously', who brought all the old familiar weaknesses of lack of knowledge and of time to a job which now really demanded professional attention.[16] Moreover the parish still remained the unit of administration – too small for economical management and subject to all the drawbacks of a tiny enclosed world dominated by personality for either good or ill.

It would have been far better to have adopted the county as the area of administration with Quarter Sessions as the supreme governing authority. Such a policy was however in 1835 politically impossible. Not only were the Benches predominantly Tory, but a Whig government could scarcely, so soon after an election, give new voting powers to a non-elective body, particularly as the county rate had been rising since the turn of the century and Quarter Sessions was already suffering unpopularity on this score. In addition there had been mounting indignation in many urban areas since the Act of 1815 which had given two Justices power summarily to close any footpath they deemed unnecessary, subject only to confirmation by Quarter Sessions. Unfortunately, and almost inevitably, certain magistrates had not been over-scrupulous in exercising this new power, and they arbitrarily abolished rights of way which interfered with the enjoyment of their estates to such an extent that even country gentlemen were raising questions in the House of Commons about the ease with which this might be done and the difficulty in getting such orders quashed. Thus it was not really possible to increase the Justices' authority over highways, and even in 1835 the immemorial autonomy of the parish was left intact to maintain the one hundred thousand miles of roads that lay outside the jurisdiction of the turnpike trusts. Between 1835 and 1850 bill after bill was brought in, in an attempt to give the magistrates in Quarter Sessions some general supervising and controlling authority, or, an even more radical suggestion, to combine them with the eleven thousand turnpike trusts and bring them all together into some unified system. That no progress at all was made along these lines reveals much about the role and development of the nineteenth-century Bench. The ultimate solution lay not in any extension of their police and magisterial jurisdiction, their historic role, but in the slowly emerging local organization for the purposes of public health which from 1848 was introducing radically new units into the old framework of county administration.

The Highways Act of 1862 empowered Quarter Sessions to divide their counties into highway districts but it left it to their discretion whether these should be based upon Poor Law unions or Petty Sessions divisions. Each new district came under a highway board composed of way wardens elected by the constituent parishes together with the Justices *ex officio*. This Act however was only permissive: some Quarter Sessions took action under the statute, others did nothing. Some adopted the Poor Law union, others the Petty Sessions divisions, and others again created entirely new areas. But the parochial opposition to the creation of these new-fangled districts was so strong that only five counties came close to abandoning the parochial system altogether. In spite of every argument of economy and efficiency in favour of wider units the parishes remained passionately attached to the management of their highways, and the diversity of action taken, the confusion of areas, and above all the vigour of the parishes prevented any sort of uniformity. Then during the 1870s the turnpike trusts began to be wound up as they got deeper and deeper into debt through failure to compete with the railways and the cost of maintaining the additional thousands of miles was at last transferred to the local authorities. No real progress was made until the Public Health Act of 1875 which created rural sanitary authorities which gradually took over the old highway boards. It really seems scarcely credible that in the England of the 1880s the surveyors of highways were still gardeners, bricklayers, broken-down clerks or merely the incompetent relations of prominent parishioners.[17]

An equally familiar aspect of Quarter Sessions business was the need to keep public order. Perhaps because it was so much part of the tradition of English life that this was a matter for the civil power, and amateur civil power at that, over most of rural England in the 1830s the peace-keeping machinery at the disposal of the local authorities consisted, much as it had done for the previous four centuries, of the high constables of the hundreds supported by the petty constables of the parishes and townships. The latter was a particularly unpopular office, involving neither status nor remuneration, and the Watching and Lighting Act of 1833 which allowed for the payment of petty constables from a rate levied by the parish overseers had unfortunately only been permissive. In 1842 an Act allowed the establishment of superintending constables, professionally trained, to supervise them in the counties which had adopted the 1833 Act. But such measures did nothing to eradicate the root of the evil: the continuing use of the parish as the unit of organization. Nor did it represent any advance upon a principle which had once made sense but had become laughable in Victorian England, that the whole community was bound to turn out to assist the peace officers in the event of a disturbance. 'Those boasted securities of self-government amounted to nothing,' exclaimed the Sheriff of Lanarkshire in disgust in 1842, probably the last man in British history to have attempted to call out the *posse comitatus*.[18]

Any real advance lay of course not with such haphazard and half-hearted measures but in the pattern established so triumphantly by Peel in his metropolitan police force. Other towns and even municipal corporations were slow to follow London's example, though the Act of 1835 required the setting up of a police force. Still in 1839 fifty-three boroughs possessed no police; and in 1848, that year of revolution, twenty-two corporate towns were still without one.[19] An ironic result of this innovation, as the Commission on County Rates pointed out as early as 1836, was that the metropolitan and borough police had driven crime into the countryside, adding yet further to the difficulties of the rural constables. As a result a Commission on the Constabulary Forces was set up, whose report, produced in 1839, firmly rejected the generally held view that poverty and distress were the great sources of crime, and said that it derived largely from the absence of any adequate police, with its corollary, the lack of any certainty of punishment, which alone in their view constituted the real deterrent. A not very successful beginning in reforming the rural police had in fact been made in Cheshire in 1829, which allowed salaried full-time constables under the control of Justices to supervise and strengthen the parish constables of their immediate districts. This had a number of disadvantages: it still failed to break away from the use of the parish unit, and more seriously it involved the magistrate in the dubious position on the one hand of virtually initiating a prosecution as head of the police and on the other of acting as judge in a case which he had himself instigated. The Police Act which finally reached the statute book in 1839 amended this in an important particular: county forces were to be under the control of Quarter Sessions, as distinct from the individual magistrate, and Quarter Sessions were also allowed to fix the strength of the force, and to appoint and dismiss the Chief Constable.

Despite this provision, which one would have expected to allay the fears of centralization and the threat of a 'French police', the 1839 Act was only adopted in just over half the counties; the others deemed it too costly a burden to impose upon the county ratepayers.[20] Many of the densely populated manufacturing districts, particularly the West Riding and the potteries, preferred to remain outside these new police arrangements, as did the great mass of rural England. It is understandable that, since it was to be organized on a county basis, the country districts should feel unwilling to foot the bill for maintaining order in the relatively distant manufacturing towns where property of high rateable value was scarce. The leaders of the opposition to what they tended to regard as unnecessary expense were all too often the magistrates themselves. Estate owners in the farming lands of the West Riding were reluctant to help provide a police force to serve Bradford, Dewsbury and Halifax. Even the efforts of Sir James Graham, who in 1842 took up the cause of police reform in the West Riding after the chaos of recent disturbances, were unavailing, and Lord Wharncliffe wrote to the Home Office in October of that year that there was not the slightest probability of a rural police force being established in the county.[21]

Only in 1856 did an Act make it compulsory for all counties to raise and organize a police force on the lines laid down in 1839, and only then was provision made for inspection, by Home Office inspectors, of all forces in the country. In the intervening years each county had gone its own way, one or two like Somerset doing nothing at all and thus becoming notorious for the length of their criminal calendar, the majority struggling to do their best with small forces and inadequate personnel and equipment. The Norfolk police in 1841 were rather ingloriously forced to detain their prisoners by chaining them to bed-posts or to mangers in stables for lack of more efficient lock-ups. In their early years the police frequently had to suffer a venomous hostility, particularly from Chartists and radicals who disliked their subordination to such an unrepresentative body as Quarter Sessions.[22] Yet in spite of some ignominious episodes when they were attacked, took refuge in the police station or actually fled the town, the police gradually came to be accepted and the idea that they represented an instrument of class domination gradually died away. By the 1850s it had become apparent that they were contributing to the improved standards of public order throughout the country. Yet still during any riots, and especially during the years of Chartist disturbance, the Justices acted on their own initiative, reading the Riot Act and swearing in special constables or, if particularly serious situations threatened, turning to the Lord Lieutenant for moral support. 'If fires and riots grow alarming the Justices of the Peace wait for the Lord Lieutenant,' wrote Sir Henry Bunbury to Lord John Russell in 1838. 'He may be an aged or an inactive man, or he may not be resident in the county; but till the Lord Lieutenant comes forward the magistrates do nothing collectively.'[23]

Although one might argue that the problems of factory labour were new (except that of course they had their origins in eighteenth-century industrial development) the Factory Act of 1833 did not mark any great step forward in the business of the Bench. The earlier factory legislation of 1802, 1819 and 1829 which had attempted to deal with the abuses of child and female labour in the textile factories had relied upon the Justices. The Act of 1833 provided for the appointment of full-time inspectors with wide powers both of regulation and prosecution, but both this and the Factory Act of 1844, although drawn up with immense care for detail, contained flaws and oversights which were exploited to the full by any magistrates whose personal interests were involved. On a dramatic occasion in 1836 when Oastler addressed a great meeting in the theatre of Blackburn, where a number of factory cases had recently been dismissed, he turned to the magistrates' box and shouted, 'You are regardless of your oaths. You are persons holding property, your only title being the law of the land. Now if the law of the land . . . is to be disregarded . . . it becomes my duty, as the guardian of the factory children, to enquire whether, in the eye of the law of England, their lives or your spindles are the most entitled to the law's protection.' Then he went on to say that if this were to happen again he would teach the children how to apply old knitting-needles to spindles 'in a way which would teach these law-defying mill-owners to have respect even to "Oastler's law", as they wrongly designated the factory law.'[24] For time and again the inspectors found that their right to order prosecutions was frustrated by the magistrates' right to impose the subsequent fines. Mill-owning magistrates were thus quite easily able to blunt the effectiveness of the 1844 Act by the ridiculously small fines they imposed, and still in 1854 Palmerston was complaining of such evasions.[25] Much of the Ten Hours Act was reduced to little more than a mockery in Lancashire where the magistrates failed to implement the legislation against relays, and dismissed cases against mills which had adopted the relay system.[26] It is perhaps not too fanciful to draw a parallel between the execution of the Factory Acts of the nineteenth century and the enclosure Acts of the sixteenth century. All went well, provided that the pockets of the individual magistrates were not too closely affected.

Thus, by the end of the 1830s, despite the activities of a reforming Whig government, the Justices were still working a familiar machine, whose essentials had changed little from the previous century. As they met at Quarter Sessions the minutes of the business before them had a familiar ring: poor, highways, prisons. The chairman still surveyed the familiar hierarchy of high and petty constables gathered in the body of the hall. True, business might go a little more smoothly now that judicial and administrative matters were dealt with separately; *ad hoc* committees were coming to be taken for granted, and even the number of standing committees was being increased, for example to deal with the constabulary. The organization of Petty Sessions continued to improve – but all this represented little more than the inevitable continuation of the changes towards a more bureaucratic Quarter Sessions which had been going on in most counties since the 1780s.

A far more significant development had been the creation of the Poor Law unions with their Boards of Guardians, for these were the first parts of an administrative jigsaw which was to be assembled piece by piece outside the immediate jurisdiction of the Justices. Already their powers had become extended as the central government recognized their potential usefulness: the Births, Deaths and Marriages Act of 1836 made the union the registration district, and from 1840 the Vaccination Act ordered Guardians to give free vaccination service. Much later still, in 1869–71, it was to become the sanitary area used by the sanitary commission. Edwin Chadwick would have liked to centre sanitary administration round the Boards of Guardians and their medical officers on the practical and sensible grounds that they were already in being and that they constituted the only machinery of local government in the county which was at the same time under adequate central supervision. But when in 1848 he finally passed his Public Health Act it introduced entirely new authorities into the local scene.[27]

The Act established a General Board of Health of three members (Viscount Morpeth, Edwin Chadwick and Lord Shaftesbury) and provided for the setting up of local Boards of Health. The establishment of these latter could be either on the petition of one tenth of the inhabitants of the area, or, where the death rate exceeded twenty-three in the thousand, by the action of the General Board which could insist on the setting up of a board by Order in Council. In corporate towns the town council became the local board; elsewhere the board was to be elected by the ratepayers, with plural voting for every £50 rate assessed. The boards might appoint their own surveyors and medical officers, but could not dismiss them without the consent of the General Board. They were to be concerned with drainage, sewers, privies; they could pave and cleanse streets; they could close burial grounds or provide public parks. This led to the creation in the local areas of a body of skilled administrators, medical officers of health, engineers, surveyors. Ultimately, that is to say before the end of the century, these men were to bring about a revolution in public health, but it must be admitted that the many compromises, which had alone secured the passage of the Bill through Parliament, reduced its effectiveness in its early days. It was normally a permissive Act, and if it was enforced in areas of a high death-rate it naturally aroused hostility among the local government officials concerned. Moreover, since it allowed a minority of ten per cent of the ratepayers to petition in disregard of the feelings and interests of the majority it could well be adopted at the price of creating a situation of bitter rivalry between the 'clean' and the 'dirty' parties.[28] In 1854 the General Board of Health came to the end of its five years' term and was subordinated by a new Act to the President and Vice-President of the Council. Four years later it was abolished, its medical duties being transferred to the Privy Council where John Simon became medical officer, its administrative duties going to the Home Office where a small local government department, the Local Government Act office, was set up to deal with the applications from the localities for the establishment of local boards.

Of the 1854 Act David Roberts has written, 'It ushered in an era of localism. . . . In the 1860's, as the *Pall Mall Gazette* later wrote, local interests held their own.'[29] This was the widespread feeling among contemporaries, and what was regarded as the triumph of localism over centralization was heralded with joy. M.P.s applauded 'the experiment of local government'; the press enthused at the prospect of an era of health administration based on 'the local knowledge, intelligence and vigour of small communities'.[30] One government inspector indeed went so far as to say that the Act 'placed before the inhabitants of every locality, for the first time in the history of our civilization, the power to do all for themselves'.[31]

The 1850s and 1860s would, one might expect, be the decades in which Victorian England proclaimed its faith in the inviolability of local government, and acted accordingly to protect and extend local liberty and independence. The actual facts are far otherwise. These years saw an immense growth of governmental interference, though it was carried out so quietly, sporadically and gradually that its cumulative effect was ignored both at the time and subsequently. This interference moreover stemmed from local demand – a demand so eager, persistent and growing that Royston Lambert reckons it a 'dynamic force'. The men of the Local Government Act office themselves were not ambitious to extend the influence of the central government, but the localities continued to refer to it frequently. The annual turnover of correspondence in the office rose from 9,814 letters in 1859 to 28,614 in 1864.[32] Petitions from local areas initiated central intervention by inquiry and report. The larger cities, it is true, still preferred to work on their own by expensive local Acts. The demand for government help came from the smaller towns and villages whose confusion about the sanitary laws encouraged them to turn to the centre for expert advice and guidance. For they recognized and appreciated the authority which the government derived simply from its superior technical skills, possessing as it did scientific knowledge, legal training and practical experience. Its wider resources and its impartial judgement gave Whitehall a compelling power in the eyes of local governors such as no legislation could ever have created.

For the Justices the 1860s were in many ways one of their best periods of government. In the 1830s they were reasonably competent by the standards of their time, and Quarter Sessions machinery was reasonably efficient after the beginnings of bureaucratic organization and the introduction of salaried officials; but their conduct of county business was often short-sighted and fumbling, for they were dealing with problems whose national implications were far beyond them. Sometimes it was their knowledge which was faulty, sometimes their insight was lacking, or they felt themselves unwilling to take on new responsibilities, but on the whole Sir John Simon's faith in the disposition of local authorities to act once they were fully and publicly informed of the situation was being justified. He held, in common with many others connected with mid-nineteenth-century central government, a genuine belief in the dynamic power of mere information. 'For him, as for so many other officials of the time, knowledge and persuasion, the exposure of abuses, and the provision of advice, seemed infinitely more preferable than coercive sanctions as a means of administration.' [33] Perhaps he was on some occasions rather too idealistic: 'The sanitary progress of the localities is almost an education matter,' he could write with an immense faith in human nature, 'wherein enlightenment counts for much more than compulsion.' It may have been an inadequate, even an illusory principle with which to launch a new era of improvement in public health, but it was a principle which augured well for the relations of central and local government. The educational effects of the succession of magnificent reports, and even more of the presence of this remarkable body of men, the government inspectors, put the Justices on their mettle and at the same time brought them guidance and advice such as they had never experienced before.

'The arrival of the inspector, an official carrying the authority of Her Majesty's Government, a personage of status and education and with a wide knowledge of facts, often turned the tide in local affairs.'[34] It was most important for the development of happy relations between central and local governments that the inspectors were the sort of men who could generally command the respect of the magistrates. They were very far removed from bureaucratic civil servants; in fact they formed almost a new intelligentsia. The great majority of them (the total was 140) came from the upper ranks of the middle class: mostly the sons of country gentry or professional men.[35] Among the assistant Poor Law Commissioners, for example, eight were magistrates themselves, and many others owned or managed landed property. They upheld the same orthodoxies as the body of men who formed the Bench of Justices, not least a sturdy Christianity and a deeply rooted moral code which emphasized 'character', and which would scorn to use its powers for unworthy ends. David Roberts has summed up their outlook:

As orthodox liberals they looked for prosperity and social improvement from the unimpeded operation of the laws of *laissez-faire*, as Christians they expected it from the moral and religious reform of the working man and as gentlemen they looked for it from the paternalism of a benevolent ruling class. Beneath these three convictions lay a belief that social progress depended not on a powerful state but on energetic, educated and morally upright individuals. Though circumstances led the inspectors to a more collectivist social outlook, they never forsook the firm foundations of Victorian individualism.[36]

Men like this would be in an excellent position to ensure that the aims of the government received a sympathetic hearing in the localities, and that the successive social reforms were presented in terms which made them acceptable to the county magistrates.

Their essential individualism, however, was soon forced to recognize that none of their ideals of improved public health, better prisons, well-regulated factories, a prosperous and contented working class, were attainable unless the direction came from the state. They were reluctantly forced into the position of saying that *laissez-faire* had its limits and that the state had a constructive role to play in general social improvements. Matthew Arnold, a school inspector, reflects this duality: like J. S. Mill he had read de Tocqueville on centralization and had acquired a fear of strong central government. Yet even while he clung to his Victorian individualism he believed in the state as a creative force and recognized the growing need for state action. Arnold is a particularly good example of the inspector at his best for he shows that it was their sense of duty, their high seriousness and their force of character which made them, wherever they went, effective beyond their mere statutory powers.[37]

The inspectors' first job was to investigate, and the great succession of reports they produced on Poor Law, mines, factories, sanitation, prisons, education are among the most important documents of nineteenth-century government. They described social conditions, they gave statistics on crime and poverty, they explained new policies, and they told of the willingness or otherwise of the local authorities to put the government regulations into effect. Most inspectors had great faith in the value of reports as a means of disseminating useful information, but they did not stop at the mere recording of evidence they had gathered. They went on to make specific recommendations, and often expounded their ideas without seeming to dictate by reporting on a model prison or workhouse in the hope that this would inspire imitation. On the whole the reports did not make exciting reading, nor did they reach a wide public, but they did reach an influential minority, the M.P.s, the local authorities and the press. Edwin Chadwick, who believed that the widest possible publicity should be given to the evils he was trying to reform, got Palmerston in 1853 to allow the General Board of Health to distribute four thousand copies of the report, and the Poor Law Board had earlier distributed eight thousand. And even those who never saw a report first hand could not have remained in ignorance of its exposures, since the daily press, pamphlets, and above all the quarterlies, made them a staple diet for their readers.[38] The great majority of Justices must have seen *The Times* even if they did not also subscribe to the *Edinburgh Review* or the *Westminster Review*. Biased of course in the weight they gave to the various reports they did none the less comment upon them, even if not always with approval. But they were unashamedly delighted in 1843 that the publicity they had given to the prison reports inspired 'our county magistrates with abject Terror, with its annual exposure of abuses in our gaols'.[39]

By the 1870s a mass of overlapping, incomplete or inconsistent statutes governed local affairs, 'a parquetry unsafe to walk upon', as Sir John Simon put it in a vivid phrase.[40] The real difficulty lay not so much in the confusing multiplicity of legislation as in the number of differing authorities supposed to execute it. This is not so very surprising when one realizes that the main consideration of the reformers had been to get things done, or at any rate begun, and the administrative means had been chosen without much thought of the pattern which would finally emerge. The pattern that had in fact emerged by the 1870s can only be described as a 'chaos of areas, a chaos of authorities and a chaos of rates'. There were in England and Wales '52 counties, 239 municipal boroughs, 70 Improvement Act districts; 1,006 urban sanitary districts, 41 port sanitary authorities, and 577 rural sanitary districts . . . 14,946 Poor Law parishes, 5,064 highway parishes not included in urban or highway districts, and about 13,000 ecclesiastical parishes'.[41]

Some progress towards unification came with the decision of the Sanitary Commission of 1869–71 that the Poor Law union was the most suitable unit for sanitary purposes, a decision which meant that it was now to become a general purpose authority, or in the phrase used by the Highways Report of 1871, 'what may be called the rural municipality'.[42] The Public Health Act of 1872 mapped out the whole country into urban and rural sanitary areas, and the official policy of consolidating local government functions within the borders of the sanitary area was carried a step further by the Highways Act of 1878 which empowered Quarter Sessions to adjust highway districts to coincide with the rural sanitary areas. Some counties, for example Wiltshire, took the further step of shaping their Petty Sessions divisions along the lines of the unions, which was to their great advantage in 1885 when the Redistribution of Seats Act employed the Petty Sessions divisions as the unit for the new electoral constituencies. The principle of a two-tier system of local government was thus being consolidated by the 1870s: the county and the sanitary district were to constitute the two basic areas. The speed at which this consolidation took place varied with the individual counties. Even in largely rural counties where new industrial growth had not complicated the picture, the situation had grown extremely confusing, almost bewildering, in its complexity. 'Fifty years of social legislation and governmental activity, on a scale and a pace never before known, had produced in Wiltshire a confusing variety of new authorities – 7 elective town councils, 6 other urban sanitary areas, 17 Poor Law unions and rural sanitary authorities, 10 highway boards, 20 or 30 burial boards, and a similar number of school boards.' [43] At the heart of the matter lay an anomaly: on the one hand the ancient county with its Bench of Justices, a virtually self-perpetuating body, standing for aristocratic principle in a world of representative bodies, and on the other, all these new authorities which had come into being since 1835, responsible to an electorate of ratepayers.

This confusion of authority was the greatest problem facing local government by the 1880s but there were others closely linked with it. Foremost was the financial question, made urgent by the great increase in the county rates which inevitably followed the unprecedented expansion of county business. The rates bore heavily upon the owners of real property, yet as one Bench pointed out,[44] the purposes for which they were levied were 'essentially of national importance and are maintained for the security of the life of all Persons equally and for the protection of every description of property' in such matters as police, prisons, asylums, coroners and the administration of justice. What made this even more bitter for the Justices to accept was that, as central direction increased in the localities, they found themselves left with only a small proportion of that sum under their immediate jurisdiction.

On the other hand the ratepayers were demanding some representation in the county authority. Small farmers and yeomen were restive at their exclusion from county government, and their clamour grew as the rates increased throughout the century. As early as 1836 Joseph Hume had proposed a bill to introduce elective county boards which would have entailed the election of councils by all ratepayers in a secret ballot. The opposition was well voiced by Lord Granville Somerset: 'It was casting an imputation upon the county magistracy which they did not deserve.'[45] This was only the first of a series of bills introduced at regular intervals during the next two or three decades and just as regularly thrown out by the House of Commons. The effect of such boards, reported a select committee in 1850 after hearing a number of witnesses, would be 'to exclude a numerous body of gentlemen in every county in England from the transaction of financial business in which as magistrates and proprietors they have immediate and extensive interests.'[46] Repeated attempts failed to persuade the House of Commons to accept the principle of the popular control of county finance. Goschen's bill of 1869 was admittedly too extreme, but its real weakness in the eyes of the landowners was that it did not include what they wanted most of all, substantial contribution to local expenses from property other than land. This, from the point of view of the Justices, was the crux of the matter. 'The argument that democratic government in the counties was intrinsically valuable had as yet been almost entirely over-shadowed in the parliamentary debates by the financial claims of owners and occupiers.'[47] A discussion of the Conservative proposal in 1878 to abolish elective county boards, recorded at the Easter sessions of the Wiltshire Bench, reveals the mind of the magistracy. They could not think, they said, that the measure was 'calculated to provide for the more efficient or economical administration of the County Funds'; it would merely mean setting up 'expensive machinery' and 'destroying the admini-strative duties of the Court of Quarter Sessions which have hitherto been performed with efficiency and economy and without the intervention of the Local Government Board.'[48] Truly, as J. S. Mill observed in 1861 in his *Considerations on Representative Government*, Quarter Sessions remained the most aristo-cratic institution in principle still in existence. He likened the Justices to feudal lords, whose important functions were theirs virtually by right of their acres, and claimed that they were in fact even more aristocratic than the House of Lords since they granted public money and disposed of important public interests not in conjunction with any popular assembly but on their own.

Quarter Sessions could not remain unreformed for ever. When the Liberals returned to power in 1880 it was quite clear that they must do something about it. If the rural workers were to get the vote, then they must also be allowed a say in their local affairs. The question of the reform of the Bench was thus linked with the question of Parliamentary franchise.[49] The issue was now quite clearly that Quarter Sessions should be made representative, or as the President of the Local Government Board, J. G. Dodson, put it in a memorandum of 1881, that an elective council should be substituted for 'a rural House of Lords in the administration of county affairs'.[50]

The Bill that introduced the County Councils was ultimately passed by the Conservatives under Lord Salisbury in 1888, largely because of pressure from their Radical allies who were led by Joseph Chamberlain. It proposed to establish in every county an elected council to which should be transferred all the financial and administrative functions of the Justices, with two exceptions, Poor Law and police. The Justices still remained *ex officio* guardians of the poor and such was their prestige that the control of the police was placed under the command of a standing joint committee of Quarter Sessions and County Council. Originally the Bill proposed that the ten largest cities should be treated as separate counties, but every town of consequence demanded a similar privilege, with the result that when the Bill was finally passed the number of county boroughs had grown to sixty-one, and what had been at first designed as exceptional became part of the general pattern of local government. The financial relief to the country gentry, who had been demanding it ever since Sir Massey Lopes fought their battles in the Commons, undoubtedly helped to make the Bill more palatable to the Justices, for it at last transferred a considerable part of the burden of taxation from the landowners to the owners of other forms of wealth.

In fact this much-dreaded, or long-desired (according to one's sympathies), constitutional revolution brought little visible change in character or in social status to the county rulers. When early in 1889 the candidates for the new councils were nominated many members of the old county families, both peers and gentry, stood for election. Very occasionally a working-class man stood but on the whole it was the men of leisure who could best afford both time and money to spend in public service. In the elections in Lincolnshire, Leicestershire and Wales it is true the tenant farmers were particularly successful, but in general the new County Council looked remarkably like the old Quarter Sessions. In Westmorland three quarters of the county councillors were magistrates; elsewhere about half the councillors also sat on the Bench, and the rest came from the same class. In 1895 exactly half the Wiltshire County Council were also Justices, and they included the Marquis of Bath, the Earls of Pembroke and Suffolk, Lord Frederick Bruce and Lord Edmond Fitzmaurice, the Hon. P. S. Wyndham and three baronets. The Marquis of Bath, the chairman of the first County Council, had been chairman of the Salisbury and Warminster sessions since 1880, while Lord Edmond Fitzmaurice, the vice-chairman, had been second chairman of the Devizes and Marlborough Sessions since 1887.[51] 'The revolution which the country gentry had resisted for half a century had in fact resulted in making them into constitutional rulers, but not in their abdication.'[52]

Why did the Justices survive so triumphantly? How could this 'rural House of Lords' still command such respect and affection, and retain such power, throughout the nineteenth century? The answer lies of course not only in the history of the Justices' own development during these years but also in the development of the landowning class itself from which they were still mostly recruited. 'The Constitution looks to property, and especially to that most stable form of property, *land*, as affording the soundest, and indeed, the only safe basis of representation and government,' said the *Quarterly Review* in 1851.[53] After the repeal of the Corn Laws Cobden and Bright wanted to go on to mobilize opinion against 'the landlord spirit which is dominant in political and social life'. They failed. 'So vast is their traditional power, so deep and ancient are its roots, so multiplied and ramified everywhere are its tendrils and creepers that the danger is never lest they shall have too little but always lest they should have too much power,' said Bernard Cracroft in 1866.[54] For the owners of the large estates seemed as strongly entrenched as ever, economically, politically and socially.

Economically, as Sir James Caird wrote in the 1870s, 'There is no other body of men in the country who administer so large a capital on their own account.' Many received large incomes from mining and from urban developments; many had well-organized estate offices; most kept up the traditionally feudal attitude towards those on their estates, for it was not until after 1875 that the relations of landlords and tenants were modified by law, the prevailing view still being that expressed by the 1833 Select Committee on Agriculture that 'the legislature can do much evil but little positive good by frequent interference with the agricultural industry'.[55] A local government return of 1876, often referred to as New Domesday Book, listed the landowners of the country and revealed the fact that as much as four fifths of the land of the United Kingdom was in the hands of no more than seven hundred peers, and of these 525 owned fifteen million acres, almost half the total acreage of the country.[56] It is possible to estimate from John Bateman's useful compilation *The Great Landowners of Great Britain and Ireland*, which derived some of its information from the owners themselves, how much land in every county was owned by the nobility. In three counties, Nottinghamshire, Wiltshire and Rutland, the proportion was over one third; elsewhere the general average was from one fifth to one seventh, though in a few it was rather less, notably in Essex where the nobility claimed only 68,000 acres out of a total of 957,000.[57]

Politically, despite the Reform Acts, little had happened to alter the basic assumption that the greatest magnates should nominate one Member of Parliament in the county in which they had a preponderant influence. The fact that the House of Lords seemed to be accepting political change, and no longer attempting to frustrate the aims of the lower house, should not be taken as an indication of their true political powers. For their strength was not as a corporate body but as individuals in their localities. As Lord Percy of Newcastle so shrewdly appreciated, there was something misleading in speaking of the English aristocracy as a 'governing class'. 'That muddleheaded phrase,' he wrote in his autobiography, 'never ceased to irritate me.' Its customary usage failed to make clear in what sense the aristocracy *was* a governing class: in his view they were not seen to advantage at Westminster, where their function was apt to be more decorative, and they relied upon the services of full-time professionals, but in the localities they came into their own. On their estates, in their native counties, the political genius of the aristocracy was seen at its best, for 'large private responsibilities do tend to form in their possessors a certain talent for public affairs'.[58]

Socially little had altered. County society still had its well-marked hierarchy, and that familiar to Lord Willoughby de Broke from the Warwickshire of his childhood would have been recognized elsewhere throughout nineteenth-century England – the only possible difference being that the place of the M.F.H. would vary with the distance from the hunting shires:[59]

THE LORD LIEUTENANT	MEMBER OF PARLIAMENT
MASTER OF FOXHOUNDS	DEAN
AGRICULTURAL LANDLORDS	ARCHDEACONS
BISHOP	JUSTICES OF THE PEACE
CHAIRMAN OF QUARTER	LESSER CLERGY
SESSIONS	LARGER FARMERS
COLONEL OF YEOMANRY	

As Bagehot recognized, deference was still strong, and there was a firm prejudice in favour of the aristocracy, and of aristocratic ideals, among all ranks and classes of the community.

Among certain sections of the aristocracy however those ideals themselves were being questioned, and the peers who played a leading role in Disraeli's 'Young England' movement proved, as Turberville has said, 'that aristocratic conservatism was capable of effulgent new ideas, of looking keenly into the future as well as maintaining the heritage of the past'.[60] In *Sybil* Charles Egremont assures the heroine that the new generation of English aristocracy will be men who fully appreciate the responsibilities of their position, who realize that their task must be approached in a serious spirit, and who, above all, once their sympathies have been awakened will prove themselves the natural, if not indeed the only, leaders of the people. This of course was Disraeli at his most romantic, but it was not without some basis in fact. In the 1850s and 1860s the aristocracy and the landowners demonstrated how much they could still feel themselves the natural leaders of society, especially of working-class society. During the years of debate on public health and sanitary reform the Radicals, though claiming to be the friends of the masses, were frequently hostile to the intervention of the government in the interests of 'improvement', whereas the landowners and capitalists, the old governing classes in whom the traditions of responsibility for the welfare of their immediate neighbourhoods were still strong, often proved to be the local leaders in the struggle for new standards. Before long the working classes began to feel that their interests were safer in their hands than in those of their professed political champions. As this became apparent so did the self-confidence and the political prestige of the old landowners return, and these decades saw something of a recovery of nerve and an access of vigour after their relative withdrawal in the 1830s. Indeed the question with which J. S. Mill opened the discussion of his *Representative Government* in 1860 – whether an efficient despotism might not be better than constitutional liberty – actually became a common subject for serious discussion during these years.[61]

'The aristocracy of England absorbs all other aristocracies and receives every man in every order and every class who defers to the principle of our society which is to aspire and to excel,' wrote Disraeli in his *Life of Lord George Bentinck*. He recognized with particular clarity the genius of the English aristocracy and the extent to which its capacity to survive depended upon its ability to change its pattern with the changing social structure and to assimilate the new forces which were emerging in an industrial world. For the Victorian industrialist or businessman, just as much as his predecessors in trade or manufacture in earlier centuries, wanted, before he died, to be considered a gentleman, and as his fortune increased 'has his eye already upon a neighbouring park, avails himself of his political position to become a country magistrate, meditates upon a baronetcy, and dreams of a coroneted descendant'.[62] The dream and desire are familiar, but the actual progress into the ranks of land-ownership was possibly both quicker and more frequent in the nineteenth century than before simply because the number of new businessmen bred by this new urban society was so vastly increased. T. H. Sweet Escott in his *Social Transformation of the Victorian Age*, published in 1897, made the suggestive comment that County Councils would not have been successful if they had been introduced before 1888. So much of their success, he believed, was due to the activity of 'this new class for the towns', wealthy commuters who had been settling themselves in the country, businessmen and industrialists with sufficient social standing, time and money to take an active part in the work of voluntary societies and local authorities. These were the men whom the county directories designated by the term 'social leaders'.[63]

Long before they actually moved into its ranks, the new industrialists were living by the standards of this aristocratic landowning society. G. M. Young asks, most pertinently, why 'in a money-making age, opinion was on the whole more deferential to birth than to money?' And he replies that the English *bourgeoisie* was essentially imitative; they had never been sufficiently isolated to frame standards of their own. The successful businessman, if he was to be regarded by himself and by others as of real consequence in the state, had to escape from the source of his wealth to acquire new interests, and 'he was more likely to magnify than to belittle the virtues of the life into which he and his wife yearned to be admitted, the life of wealth, of power and consideration on the land'.[64] To put it at its lowest: Englishmen have always been snobs. But this is unnecessarily cynical. As Carlyle recognized, combined with 'a certain vulgarly human admiration' for the aristocracy went 'a spontaneous recognition of their good qualities and good fortune, which is by no means wholly envious or wholly servile', and he concluded that, in spite of lamentable exceptions, 'there was still no class among us intrinsically so valuable and recommendable'.[65]

Both the continued vigour of the 'deference society' and the recruitment into it of the *nouveaux riches* had important consequences for the Bench of Justices. It meant, in the first place, that the Justices were still accepted without question as the local governors of their counties, and the central government had no option but to recognize this. Sir James Graham, for example, himself a former county magistrate, saw his scheme of employing salaried assistant barristers to aid Quarter Sessions shelved on the grounds that it would have the effect of 'depriving the gentry of property and education of their influence in the several counties in which they reside'.[66] But it also meant that the county Benches were able to reflect the structure of the counties they served. In a basically rural county of course where changes came only slowly the Bench would still be predominantly landed. In 1876 in Lincolnshire, for example, there were still only 183 magistrates for the county[67] and the Post Office Directory for that year illustrates the extent to which this remained the government of an élite, for among them there were fifty-five clergymen, six peers, seven sons of peers, seven baronets and eight M.P.s. Wiltshire similarly had a very strong tradition of ruling county families and an active resident aristocracy, so that it is scarcely surprising to find that among the 203 qualified to act as Justices in March 1875 there should be one duke, three marquises, four earls, four barons, ten close relatives of peers, thirteen baronets, two knights, twenty-four clergymen, and 142 squires.[68] Here of course the long tradition of the west of England textile industry meant that the manufacturer was scarcely distinguishable from his neighbouring squire.

This was also true in other parts of the country. John Howard, Justice for Cheshire, ran a mill at Hyde but lived in a magnificent Elizabethan mansion, Brereton Hall. In 1863 Lord Braybrooke recommended for admission to the Essex Bench the 'head of a very large Drug factory' whose main qualification was that he was a 'keen fox hunter'.[69] But on the northern Benches, in Lancashire and Yorkshire particularly, the mill-owning industrialist magistrates stood apart from their fellows. They certainly existed in sufficient numbers for serious consideration to be paid to a proposal made in connexion with Ashley's Factory Reform Bill to prevent them hearing cases arising from it, a suggestion which Nassau Senior thought would 'leave the enforcement of the Act to the clergy and country gentlemen –

classes generally opposed to the millowners in habits and politics, and without practical knowledge of the system'.[70] But Senior seems to have been unduly pessimistic here.

A closer study of one individual Bench which represented both agricultural and industrial interests shows that the two classes shared a common outlook both with regard to county affairs in general and to the conduct of business at Quarter Sessions in particular. J. M. Lee has made a most valuable investigation of the Bench in Cheshire at the end of the nineteenth century. The central theme of his study is that by the 1880s a new county society had been created, and that Quarter Sessions reflects this. *Walford's County Families* for 1879 lists over 250 families for Cheshire, of whom 235 were resident, and of these barely one hundred are clearly identifiable as gentry with a considerable landed estate, and at least seventy-three are merchants or manufacturers.[71] He points out that the *appearance* of government by the landed gentry was retained and the aristocratic landowners still played a leading role in county affairs; the family names which appear on Quarter Sessions orders in the 1840s are still there forty years later.[72] The transition was made easier by the fact that the really large landowners thought in the same terms as the industrialists: investing in urban development, welcoming the coming of the railways, having a London house or club. In Cheshire, at least, Quarter Sessions in the 1880s was ruled by a class of successful business people presided over by the great landowners or county political patrons.[73]

As always in speaking of the composition of the Bench, generalizations are dangerous. The Lord Lieutenants still controlled entry to the magistracy and the type of man they accepted for their counties reflected their personal idiosyncrasies. Their main prejudices lay against Dissenters and industrialists. The Duke of Newcastle, Lord Lieutenant of Nottinghamshire, was actually deprived of office by the Whigs in 1839 for pressing his objections to a Mr Paget, 'First because he was a man of violent political opinions; and, secondly, because he was a Dissenter.'[74] A Home Office correspondent attributed the shortage of magistrates in the Hinckley district of Leicestershire in the same year to the Lord Lieutenant's habit of using the commission of the peace as a political prize. Certainly the Duke of Portland's reluctance to recommend reformers to the Middlesex commission was well known. Perhaps more surprisingly one or two counties still persisted in excluding clergy, a short-sighted policy which succeeded only in reducing the number of resident magistrates, generally in areas in which they were most greatly needed. The Duke of Portland complained of the difficulties this caused in Derbyshire: 'I live within a mile of the borders of that county and when I am from home, parties are sometimes obliged to go twelve or thirteen miles to get their business done.'[75]

The unequal distribution of magistrates was still, as it had always been, one of the most serious weaknesses of English local government. In 1839, for example, when Chartist disturbances were expected at Middleton precautionary measures were impossible because there was no one to swear in any special constables. The nearest magistrates were at Manchester, Bury, Oldham and Ashton-under-Lyne, that is to say, anything from four to seven miles distant. Even if a resident magistrate were available he might not be equal to the demands of his office, as when riots started at Wigton in Cumberland in 1842, and the only magistrate there was too infirm to patrol the streets.

Such situations were bound to arise while the Justices remained amateurs appointed in an entirely haphazard and unsystematic way, but the inadequate behaviour of the active magistrate is more difficult to excuse. They were of course subject to all the human infirmities, not least bad temper.[76] Napier's scathing remarks are perhaps a little extreme: 'The county magistrates are a miserable set generally; they insult the people, are hated, and on every alarm grow frightened.'[77] But there are certainly some startling examples of neglect of duty: of magistrates who went grouse shooting during the 1839 Chartist disturbances, or who failed to send in reports of meetings even when addressed by such inflammatory leaders as Stephens and O'Connor. A particularly serious weakness was their tendency to disappear from the scene when the troops arrived – thus making a mockery of the Home Office insistence that military force should be used only under the direction of the civil powers. What Mather has called 'the Peterloo touch' was still there, a tendency to panic, to go to extremes of severity and to ride roughshod over civil liberties in situations which were nothing like as dangerous as they imagined.

Is it possible to make any useful generalizations at all about the character and conduct of the Justices in the nineteenth century? The conclusion that the magistracy while not over-conscientious were generally competent is safe but not very illuminating. Perhaps it might be more worth while to attempt to ask of them the question that is constantly asked of the central government during this period. To what extent was their administration guided by the utilitarian principles enunciated by Jeremy Bentham and his disciples?

It is of course necessary to establish in the first place that they would be aware of what Benthamism demanded by way of social and administrative reform. It has been said earlier in this chapter that the publicity given to government reports and the presence of government inspectors in the localities would bring them frequently into contact with the Benthamite ideas.[78] If even Sidney Smith could boast that he had read all of Bentham and the Irish radical Daniel O'Connell could call himself a disciple,[79] one can only suppose that his writings found their way into very varied corners of Victorian society. But did the county magistrates think in these terms at all? Why did they, for example, accept the new Poor Law? Was it because they were deeply convinced of the principles upon which it was based? Or was it not simply that they realized it was a chance to rid themselves of a great many burdensome rates and even more burdensome duties? Accepting a certain amount of centralization was only a small price to pay for securing lower poor-rates on their property. And, as Halévy has pointed out, in allowing the radical doctrinaires to dispossess them of this most important part of their administrative duties they in fact escaped the unpopularity which inevitably followed a more strict interpretation of the law. In the violent campaign in the north against the new Poor Law the agitators held up the previous regime of the overseers controlled by the Justices as a sort of golden age now gone for ever. Their loss of administrative power was small compared with what they gained in moral influence.[80]

The same might be said of each new administrative development in turn. Most magistrates, in whom the traditions of social responsibility were strong, could recognize and approve attempts to reform society and particularly to ameliorate the lot of the lower orders, but their altruism was not always strong enough to override their economic interests. Counties would hesitate to establish a police force when they saw how costly it would prove; mill-owning magistrates would frustrate the best intentions of the factory reformers if they themselves could gain by it. As in every other age the Justices of the Peace were the willing and effective servants of the central government whenever it suited them to be so.

References

1. Quoted J. T. Ward, *The Factory Movement 1830–1855*, Macmillan, 1962, p. 122.
2. For further reading on this, see J. E. O'Neill, 'Finding a Policy for the Sick Poor', *Victorian Studies*, 1964, VII, No. 3, p. 262, and D. Roberts, 'How Cruel was the Victorian Poor Law?', *Historical Journal*, 1963, VI, pp. 97–107.
3. G. M. Young and K. Hancock, *English Historical Documents 1833–1874*, Eyre & Spottiswoode, 1956, p. 922.
4. Quoted *Chartist Studies*, ed. Asa Briggs, Macmillan, 1959, p. 1.
5. D. Roberts, *Victorian Origins of the British Welfare State*, Yale Historical Publications, 1960, p. 324.
6. Review of Roberts's note cited above, in *Victorian Studies*, 1961, IV, No. 3, pp. 261.
7. Roberts, *Victorian Origins*, p. 100.
8. *Government by Commissioners*, 1849, p. 367, quoted Roberts, *op. cit.*, p. 100.
9. Roberts, *op. cit.*, p. 303.
10. See R. M. Gutchen, 'Local Improvements and Centralisation in Nineteenth Century England', *Historical Journal*, 1961, IV, pp. 85–96.
11. See H. Parris, 'The Nineteenth Century Revolution in Government: A Reappraisal Reappraised', *Historical Journal*, 1960, I, pp. 17–37.
12. Quoted Roberts, *op. cit.*, p. 47.
13. *ibid.*, p. 24.
14. *ibid.*, pp. 47–8.
15. R.A. Lewis, 'County Government since 1835', *V.C.H. Wiltshire*, 1957, V, p. 242.
16. *ibid.*, p. 248.
17. S. and B. Webb, *English Local Government: The Story of the King's Highway*, Longmans, 1913, p. 211.

18. Quoted F. C. Mather, *Public Order in the Age of the Chartists*, Manchester University Press, 1959, p. 81.
19. See Mather, *op. cit.*, Chapter IV, 'The New Police', *passim*, and J. M. Hart, 'The Reform of the Borough Police 1835–1856', *English Historical Review*, 1955, LXX.
20. In Wiltshire the establishment of a police force in 1839 led at once to the doubling of the rates. From Michaelmas 1840 the county levied a special police rate which equalled, and in some years exceeded, the amount of the county rate for all other purposes.
21. Mather, *op. cit.*, p. 132.
22. *ibid.*, p. 137.
23. Quoted Mather, *op. cit.*, p. 53.
24. Ward, *op. cit.*, p. 161.
25. Roberts, *op. cit.*, p. 109.
26. Ward, *op. cit.*, p. 356.
27. Young and Hancock, *op. cit.*, p. 757.
28. The issues roused deep feeling, and were not without their political, economic and religious bearings. They cannot be fully discussed here, but see Young and Hancock, *op. cit.*, pp. 758–9, and S. E. Finer, *Life and Times of Sir Edwin Chadwick*, Methuen, 1952, pp. 431–9.
29. Roberts, *op. cit.*, p. 95.
30. Royston Lambert, 'Central and Local Relations in mid-Victorian England. The Local Government Act Office, 1858–1871', *Victorian Studies*, 1962, VI, No. 12, pp. 123–4.
31. *ibid.*, p. 123.
32. *ibid.*, p. 133.
33. R. J. Lambert, *Sir John Simon and English Social Administration*, Macgibbon & Kee, 1963, p. 264.
34. Roberts, *op. cit.*, p. 308.
35. The background of the inspectors is analysed in detail by Roberts, *ibid.*, pp. 152 ff.
36. *ibid.*, pp. 168–9.
37. *ibid.*, p. 702.
38. See Roberts, *ibid.*, pp. 228–31.
39. Quoted Roberts, *ibid.*, p. 230.
40. Lambert, *Sir John Simon*, p. 501.
41. Young and Hancock, *op. cit.*, p. 615.
42. Lewis, *op. cit.*, p. 258.
43. *ibid.*, p. 263.
44. *ibid.*, p. 262.
45. B. Keith-Lucas, *The English Local Government Franchise*, Oxford University Press, 1952, p. 98.
46. *ibid.*, p. 101.
47. *ibid.*, p. 105.
48. Lewis, *op. cit.*, p. 263.
49. See Keith-Lucas, *op. cit.*, pp. 107 ff.

50. Quoted Keith-Lucas, *ibid.*, p. 107.
51. Lewis, *op. cit.*, p. 265.
52. Keith-Lucas, *op. cit.*, p. 115.
53. Quoted Asa Briggs, *The Age of Improvement*, Longmans, 1959, p. 406, note 2.
54. *ibid.*, p. 406.
55. *ibid.*, p. 407, note 3.
56. A. S. Turberville, 'Aristocracy and the Advent of Democracy, 1837–1876', epilogue to *The House of Lords in the Age of Reform, 1784–1837*, Faber, 1958, p. 408.
57. *ibid.*, p. 409.
58. D. Spring, 'The Role of the Aristocracy in late nineteenth century', *Victorian Studies*, 1960, IV, No. 1, p. 57.
59. Quoted H. J. Hanham, *Elections and party management: politics in the time of Disraeli and Gladstone*, Longmans, 1959, p. 4.
60. Turberville, *op. cit.*, p. 398.
61. Young and Hancock, *op. cit.*, 759.
62. Quoted Briggs, *op. cit.*, p. 408.
63. J. M. Lee, *Social Leaders and Public Persons. A Study of County Government in Cheshire since 1888*, Oxford University Press, 1963, pp. 5–7.
64. *Early Victorian England, 1830–1865*, ed. G. M. Young, Oxford University Press, 1934, II, p. 486. Quoted Turberville, *op. cit.*, p. 427.
65. *Critical and Historical Essays*, 1840, V, p. 14. Quoted Turberville, *op. cit.*, p. 427.
66. Mather, *op. cit.*, pp. 64–5.
67. Hanham, *op. cit.*, p. 3.
68. Lewis, *op. cit.*, p. 232.
69. F. M. L. Thompson, *English Landed Society in the Nineteenth Century*, Routledge, 1963, p. 288.
70. Ward, *op. cit.*, p. 170.
71. Lee, *op. cit.*, p. 23.
72. *ibid.*, p. 18.
73. *ibid.*, p. 22.
74. Quoted Mather, *op. cit.*, p. 55.
75. *ibid.*, p. 57.
76. See *ibid.*, p. 60.
77. *ibid.*, p. 58.
78. The extent to which Edwin Chadwick was in fact influenced by Bentham is debatable. For a discussion of what Chadwick owed to Bentham, see S. E. Finer, *op. cit.*, pp. 12–37; but cf. D. Roberts, 'Jeremy Bentham and the Victorian Administrative State', *Victorian Studies*, 1958, II, No. 3, pp. 193–211.
79. Roberts, *Victorian Origins*, p. 198.
80. E. Halévy, 'Before 1835', *A Century of Municipal Progress*, eds. H. J. Laski, W. Ivor Jennings and W. A. Robson, Allen & Unwin, 1935, p. 35.

CHAPTER SEVEN

The Borough Justices

'SUMMA RUSTICITAS, the pig was ubiquitous.... In Cambridge, even under Elizabeth, there was a strong smack of the farmyard.'[1] But even though Maitland was undoubtedly right in some respects, the fact remains that the borough Justices and the Quarter Sessions in the towns were very different affairs from their counterparts in the countryside. Legislation made no distinction, it is true, between the corporate Justice and the county Justice, but although they found themselves dealing with the same crimes and executing the same statutes the similarity ended there. The first, and the most fundamental, difference lay in their constitution. Only in a few exceptional boroughs, such as Oxford, Poole or Haverfordwest, was a separate commission of the peace issued, which would include a number of local dignitaries, who generally did not attend, as well as the leading members of the corporation. Elsewhere the Quarter Sessions for the boroughs were held under the authority of the borough charter which established those members of the corporation, mayor, aldermen, bailiff, recorder and so on, who were to constitute the Bench. Thereafter this small and oligarchical group co-opted new members when necessary without further outside interference. Numbers on any urban Bench therefore tended to be small, generally speaking no more than three or four: the mayor together with two or three aldermen. Typical was High Wycombe, where the Bench was made up of the mayor, the ex-mayor and the recorder, or Walsall, where it consisted of the mayor together with two of the 'most ancient Capital Burgesses'. A charter of 1610 to Stratford on Avon empowered the chief alderman with the bailiff and the recorder to hold a court of Quarter Sessions in the guildhall, but a subsequent charter of 1664 increased the number to five.[2] Southampton had an exceptionally high total of eleven Justices, but then the Bishop of

Winchester never sat nor did the two Justices chosen from among the burgesses in general.

The privilege of holding its own Quarter Sessions was much sought after and was indeed one of the motive forces in the determination of many towns to secure a charter. The main attraction lay in the right to exclude the county Justices and to enjoy immunity from the jurisdiction of the county Bench. The inhabitants of Deal described the situation bluntly in 1698: 'that they are obliged to go to . . . Sandwich whenever they need a Justice of the Peace . . . Sandwich monopolizes all law and justice.'[3] The jubilation which greeted the acquisition of the new freedom is typified by the rejoicings in Lincoln at the arrival of the new charter on 1 January 1685 when the mayor and corporation walked in state to the guildhall where he was sworn mayor and Justice of the Peace amidst general acclaim while the conduits ran with claret.[4] 'The Justices of the Peace for the county shall not hereafter in any wise intermeddle with the said city or liberties thereof.'[5] The phrase rings out grandly: the reality was often rather less impressive. This exemption from their jurisdiction was often resented and sometimes actually resisted by the county Justices, and might lead to much unedifying wrangling between the two authorities. In cases of bitter internal strife, such as that at Walsall between the borough proper and other parts of the town, the county Justices would ally themselves with the opponents of the borough and thus gain a foothold from which to try and reassert their influence.[6]

The Webbs estimate that by 1689 there were about two hundred borough Benches and more were created during the following century. The bewildering complexity which characterizes urban history in general is evident here too. 'England in very ancient times was productive of cunning framers of constitutions,' wrote a learned antiquarian in 1832, 'very few towns in England are governed by the same laws; and while many of them have whimsical, many more have exceedingly beautiful forms of government.'[7] The successive gradations of jurisdiction complicate any general estimation of 'just what any town actually gained by the right to hold its own sessions. At the top of the municipal hierarchy came the nineteen counties corporate which totally excluded the county Bench and were directly responsible to the Crown for all duties except that of the militia, for which they came under the Lord Lieutenant. Below this came varying degrees of emancipation from county jurisdiction: forty corporations had in effect no more than the powers of Petty Sessions, that is to say, the right to deal with minor assaults and nuisances, while a number of other boroughs had gained the right to exclude the county Justices for graver felonies. By 1835, in addition to the nineteen counties corporate, forty other boroughs also excluded the county Bench and ninety-nine had a jurisdiction substantially separate from that of the county. Only in thirty-five boroughs did the borough Justices have concurrent jurisdiction with the county Bench which allowed them to hold special and Petty Sessions. Towns did of course move from one category to another, and although it was more usual to seek additional privileges one town at least was willing to forgo a privilege for reasons of economy. Until 1725 Southampton was one of these towns which in addition to Quarter Sessions held regular sessions of oyer and terminer and gaol delivery in which they could even try cases of treason should they arise. But in that year, pressed by debt and anxious to economize, they adopted the practice of applying for inclusion in the western circuit of the Assize Judges whenever there were any prisoners charged with offences which required a trial at Assizes.[8]

If it is difficult to be precise about the organization of the borough sessions it is even more difficult to try to talk about the men who actually ran the Benches. The borough Justices were in fact simply the local town officials, a small coterie of those men who held the principal offices in the borough. By occupation they would be tradesmen, bakers, grocers, maltsters, chapmen and so on, with representatives of whatever was the dominant industry of the town. In cathedral towns the bishop and a prebendary or two might be included, in Oxford and Cambridge a number of members of the university; but in general the borough Justice was a small man – and there was perhaps more than a hint of self-importance in a seventeenth-century custom, found in some places, of setting up ornamented 'magistrates' posts' outside the houses of those who sat on the borough Bench.

Although there were undoubtedly disadvantages, as Burke recognized, in having magistrates drawn from such social classes, a much more serious drawback was the tendency, apparent at an early date, for the borough Justices to develop into a small, self-perpetuating oligarchy. The very machinery of the appointment to the Bench encouraged this since it ensured that it should be confined to the small circle connected with the corporation. An excellent example of how exclusive this was likely to be comes from Macclesfield where it was the practice for the common burgesses to elect annually five capital burgesses, who then elected from their number the mayor and two aldermen for the following year, who, at the same time that they were sworn, were constituted Justices for their term of office and for the following year.[9] Almost inevitably these men would grow away from their local communities until by the early nineteenth century they had become pretty well detached from the general body of the inhabitants. Thus at a time when the population of Walsall was between six and seven thousand the magistracy was falling into fewer and fewer hands, and was at the same time finding it increasingly difficult to command the respect of the populace at large. Known derisively as 'the Rump' the local Bench at this time was characterized, in the words of the historian of Walsall, by 'bankruptcy of members and moral decadence'.[10]

If the balance sheet is to be made out fairly, it must be reckoned in their favour that the borough Benches always included among their magistrates a recorder, a barrister 'learned in the law', who provided sessions with an element of trained professional competence often lacking in their equivalents in the counties. Southampton actually went so far as to remove a recorder whom it considered was doing his job unworthily. The quality of his successor is demonstrated by the fact that he resigned the office after twenty years on becoming chief baron of the Court of Exchequer.[11]

The strength of the borough Justices, based on the smallness of their numbers and the oligarchical nature of their constitutions, was increased by the common habit of holding frequent adjourned sessions. Often by the eighteenth century they would be meeting fortnightly or even weekly, as at Coventry where the

Justices met every Friday by adjournment in the mayor's parlour, or at Leeds where the mayor with one or two aldermen sat twice a week as Petty Sessions. The comparatively small area which came under their jurisdiction also enhanced their authority, particularly when, as was often the case, this was further sub-divided so that each borough magistrate had special oversight of one area or district of the town, as in London, Bristol and Norwich, which allocated men to particular wards. In addition, and this was a definite advantage over their colleagues in the counties, the borough Justices enjoyed the services of paid subordinates, salaried beadles and watchmen, a force of deputy constables for watch and ward, possibly scavengers and street keepers. And of course they always had the borough gaol close at hand to receive offenders.

The relation of the borough Justices to other corporate bodies varied from place to place. In some, Quarter Sessions soon began to gain supremacy over all the other urban authorities. One service after another which had originally been organized and paid for by the municipal corporation came into their hands. It was as Justices and not as the council that in many towns the mayor and aldermen kept control of the corporate property, and it was as Justices that they gave orders for watch, directed constables, instructed surveyors and controlled overseers. The early eighteenth-century Quarter Sessions minutes at Westminster show not only the Justices' control of alehouses, vagrants, over-seers and surveyors, but also their encroachment upon the duties of the court of burgesses in such matters as the watch or paving and cleansing the streets, until by the middle years of the century the burgesses had little left but 'a shadow of power'.[12] This did not happen everywhere, however. The fact that in 1696 it was necessary at Walsall to pass an ordinance ordering that the mayor should hold Quarter Sessions or else pay to the burgesses a capital sum of £10 suggests that the court was hardly yet an integral part of town government.[13] At High Wycombe the com-mon council continued to supervise all aspects of public life in the town, and even such matters as the Poor Law which should have been subject to the borough J.P.s still remained under their control.[14] Once instituted, it is true that Quarter Sessions did generally survive somehow, if only to proclaim the borough's right to an independent jurisdiction in terms which could be understood by an age for which the Bench of Justices was the really authoritative instrument of local government. But how little it contributed to municipal affairs can be seen at High Wycombe where, apart from appointing such officials as flesh-tasters, aletasters and leathersealers, whose duties were by then purely nominal, it was meeting from 1769 no more than once a year and if it did perform any judicial functions these are not recorded. 'In many ways it was the institutional equivalent of a new-built eighteenth-century "Gothick" ruin, using the forms of the Middle Ages but bearing the stamp of its own day and contrived more for ornament than use.'[15]

The years between 1750 and 1834 have many claims to be called the years of municipal anarchy. They saw adaptations and experiments (particularly in the form of the Improvement Commissioners), but these amounted to little more than slight modifications to a system that was basically tyrannous and corrupt, and totally inadequate to deal with the pressures of urban life at the end of the eighteenth century. England in the 1780s was still an agricultural land: the village was a more familiar social unit than either town or city. In 1800 no more than about 20 per cent of the population was urban, but from 1800 to 1850 the rate of growth in the towns increased dramatically. By 1851 the urban population of Britain just outnumbered the rural; by 1861 the proportion stood at five to four; by 1861 the urban was more than double the rural. Statistics provide the bald outline; within it lie infinitely varied patterns of urban development. Manchester at the beginning of the eighteenth century was a town of 8,000; between the late 1780s and the first census of 1801 it grew from 40,000 to over 70,000, until in 1831 when it had become a town of 142,000 it could claim that its population had multiplied nearly six times in sixty years. In 1801 Halifax and Blackburn both had a population of 12,000; by 1831 the former stood at 24,000, the latter at 27,000 and in the following twenty years went up to 65,000. Sheffield grew from 46,000 in 1801 to 92,000 in 1831. The rate of growth at Bradford after 1815 was described with pride as 'one of the most striking phenomena in the history of the British Empire': in no decade between 1811 and 1851 did the increase fall below 50 per cent. So much is apparent simply from the census returns; the figures make clear a point that needs to be emphasized again and again, that it was not the size of towns but the rate of their growth which was so unparalleled. It was this which lay at the root of the troubles of urban local government during these years. It used to be said of Birmingham at the end of the eighteenth century that the traveller might 'chance to find a street of houses in the autumn where he last saw his horse at grass in the spring'.[16] Speed such as this made questions of public health and public order of urgent importance, but it was not until the Municipal Reform Act of 1835 that the towns were given the mechanism with which to begin to deal efficiently with their social problems. After eighty years of violent, sometimes alarming industrialization, many northern and midland towns found themselves with a legacy of slum housing, inadequate sanitation, sickly children and all the evils of human wretchedness and squalor which go with overcrowding and lack of planning for a vast labour influx.

The problems of the new towns are striking: we are unlikely to forget the Coketown of Dickens's *Hard Times* or 'the insensate industrial town' of Lewis Mumford's castigations. We may forget however that these years were just as difficult for the less fortunate, less active towns which industrial and commercial prosperity passed by. The failure of the municipal Justices is not only their more obvious failure in the towns of the industrial revolution; it is their equally important though less noticed degeneration in the small cathedral and market towns up and down the country. The years before 1835, wrote J. L. Hammond, with only a slight exaggeration of the truth, saw the towns of England sunk in a condition of barbarism that would have put a citizen of the Roman Empire to the blush. 'They had none of the amenities, few of the decencies of civilization.'

The only mitigating circumstance of these years lay in the passing of Improvement Acts which invested commissioners with powers to deal with particular matters such as sanitation, lighting, drainage and police. The creation of these new statutory authorities added even more to the already great confusion of existing local powers. Membership might be by nomination, election or co-option; revenue might come from tolls, rates, dues or subscriptions. They might or might not add to the powers of the borough Justices, depending upon whether the magistrates were themselves commissioners or not. They would in any case add considerably to the number of bye-laws which the Justices were bound to enforce. Usually their financial powers were strictly limited; often any really large-scale schemes were frustrated by private interest; in nearly all cases they concentrated upon the central and more attractive residential areas and neglected the working-class districts and the potential slums. But despite their limitations, and despite a general tendency to succumb to vested interests, these Improvement Commissioners did manage to carry out reforms which would otherwise never have materialized.

Their basic weakness, which they shared with the long-standing borough Justices, was a fundamental one. The tie which had originally bound the corporation burgesses together had been their common ownership of land and their common interests as traders and craftsmen. Such an outlook died hard, and as a result the eighteenth-century municipal corporation 'regarded itself far less as an instrument of local government of the modern type than as an institution for the management of a corporate property'. In the past they had consented to regulate local trade and industry, but when *laissez-faire* rendered this obsolete 'there followed a hiatus in which they remained blissfully unaware that there was anything much for them to do'.[17] Thus their view of what constituted *improvement* was essentially a limited one: it meant increasing the security of their property. The great majority of Improvement Commissioners were not really interested in public health *per se*; they turned their attention to pavements or lighting mainly because it would increase the comfort and safety of their own persons. They concentrated on such matters as bonfires and coal-carts but on the whole left the really big problems untouched. Even the provision of rudimentary social services was subordinated to the interests of the management of property and the maintenance of privilege.[18]

Life was made difficult for the borough magistrates at this time by the anomalies in the extent and area of their jurisdiction. In 1792 there was not a single magistrate in the town of Sheffield. One lived fourteen miles away, the other 'having made some efforts during the riots last year relative to some enclosures, the populace burned part of his property, and since that time he has been very little in the country'.[19] In most of the ancient boroughs by the early nineteenth century there were enclaves of territory wholly or partly exempt from the authority of the borough magistrates. With rapid urban growth the uncertain geographical limits of their authority could become a serious matter. What was the relation of the municipal borough to the new areas which now enclosed it? For almost certainly the suburban growth took place outside the limits of the jurisdiction originally granted to the borough Bench in their charter. Leicester at the end of the eighteenth century witnessed the bitter disputes and litigation to which such questions gave rise.[20]

Another weakness of the borough magistracy was the comparatively short period of their term of office, which made it even more difficult for them than it was for the county Justices to sustain a concerted policy for any length of time. During the mayoralty of a chief magistrate who was more energetic and public-spirited than average there would be a burst of activity, but under his successor everything might be allowed to lapse. Thus the spirited exertions of John Eames in Leicester brought about the issue of admonitions to constables, headboroughs, nightwatchmen and licensed victuallers to be more assiduous in their duties; deficient weights and measures were seized and burnt or broken; proclamations were made about Sabbath observance and fair trading. But all this bore the impress of one man, and that faded as quickly as his own rule.[21]

For the fundamental failure of the old system was the failure of men. In some places there was no longer the full complement of magistrates since, as one mayor confessed, small tradesmen preferred to pay a fine rather than fulfil an office which was a burden too great to bear. 'There is not a single man in the place,' wrote a Devonshire J.P. indignantly of the borough of Bradnich, 'who has the education which would fit him for the lowest station of a clerk in a counting-house of a decent manufacturer.

On all occasions, except at Quarter Sessions when an attorney presides, the law is attempted to be spelt out of an edition of Burn fifty years old.'[22] Most notorious of all was Joseph Merceron in Bethnal Green who from the 1780s as an active Justice and virtually dictator of the parish was totally unscrupulous in building up an empire for himself. 'The rule of this Boss,' write the Webbs, 'for a whole generation as complete and as equivocal as that of a Tammany leader of New York City, was fortified by the multiplicity of his honorary appointments.'[23] The picture is an alarming one: he was able to appoint complacent overseers whose accounts, practically all of his own expenditure, he always passed; he would always secure the renewal of licences to public houses of his supporters however disreputable; he was quite prepared to alter the rate-books in order to reduce his supporters' rates; he was not above gaining popularity for himself by his toleration of dog-fighting and bullock-hunting in the streets despite the protests of the more respectable inhabitants. The really startling aspect of his regime is that despite the opposition of a public-spirited rector he continued in more or less undisputed supremacy for at least half a century. A Parliamentary Commission in 1830 inquired again into the parish government; the complaints were the same – corruption, partiality of assessments, jobbery and secret expenditure. Yet nothing was reformed. The misrule of the sanctimonious and corrupt Mainwaring family on the Middlesex Bench reveals a similar situation. For forty years the Bench was made up of dishonest tradesmen: the Mainwarings introduced a widespread system of corruption and managed simultaneously to receive a secret pension from the government and to make a large profit from their control of local funds.

The inadequacy of such men was shown up most glaringly when they were faced with the town mob – an occurrence only too frequent at the end of the eighteenth century and in the opening years of the nineteenth. Disturbances were often caused by industrial unrest, but they might also be sparked off by the high price of bread, by political discontent, or even, as Wesley's journals record, by religious rivalries, with the aim of 'destroying the Methodists'. In such situations the borough magistrates found the system of watch and ward inadequate; they did not

176

want to rely on the military nor did they want to turn to the county Bench, and lessen their own authority. Often the borough gaol proved too small, sometimes too unsafe, to hold even the ringleaders. Small tradesmen were the last people likely to be able to bring their personal authority to bear on rioting workers. The country Justice could still command respect since he generally knew and understood the men he had to govern, and since he still had some kind of natural authority over them in a society in which deference remained part of the accepted order of things. In the towns things were very different, and the failure of government could not, by its very nature, be hidden from the public eye. The more or less total abdication of the Bristol Bench during the riots of 1831 proved once and for all how impossible it was to entrust borough magistrates with matters as serious as these. Bristol after all was a city of considerable size and importance, ranking as the third seaport in the kingdom in the eighteenth century. The duties of its magistrates had grown so numerous that the mayor and aldermen were supposed to meet for two hours daily in Quarter Sessions, but by this time they were no longer really concerned about their responsibilities. Most of them had bought themselves fine country houses on the outskirts of the city and many never came near their magisterial duties, allowing the supervision of their respective wards to lapse into more or less total neglect. Perhaps they found the Gloucestershire Bench more attractive, since it carried with it the entrée into the landowning world for which they longed.[24] To membership of an urban Bench no such status was attached.

The example of Leeds, where there was a Bench of men at once honest and enterprising but which had still by the 1830s become the object of hostility in the city, illustrates only too vividly how pitifully inadequate urban government was even where it was well intentioned. The Leeds Justices consisted of the mayor and twelve aldermen, an oligarchical group recruiting themselves from among the leading Church of England families. As more and more of the government of the town came into their hands they dealt with the extension of their business, which followed from the rapid growth of population, with a great show of efficiency. In the later eighteenth century their bye-laws concerning traffic, licensing and so on were excellent; they established a police court or 'rotation office' at which two of them in turn attended to cases. Yet they remained distrusted and disliked: distrusted because they excluded so many from the Bench by reason of their religion or their politics, and because of the traditional secrecy of the magistrates' proceedings; disliked because of the heavy poor rates they imposed. The radical Dissenters, determined to fight against their exclusion from the Bench, gained control of the vestry and began a battle with the magistrates over poor relief and highway maintenance, until by the 1830s Leeds presented the unedifying spectacle of a town in which the machinery of local government had ceased to function in spite of the honesty of all the parties concerned.

When Lord Althorp introduced his bill to reform municipal corporations in 1833 he told the House of Commons that the borough magistracy had forfeited all public confidence. By the 1830s the demands for reform had grown more vociferous. The repeal of the Test and Corporation Acts in 1828 made the Dissenters even more impatient at their exclusion from local government by what one Whig newspaper called 'a shabby mongrel aristocracy'. The successful manufacturers and merchants, able, prosperous and energetic, felt bitter about the composition of the urban Benches; the country gentlemen looked askance at these little islands of corrupt and degenerate privilege in the midst of their native counties. Their protests bore fruit in the appointment in 1833 of a Royal Commission to examine municipal corporations which within eighteen months investigated the constitutions and workings of hundreds of corporations throughout the country. The report which the twenty commissioners produced has come in for much criticism. The Webbs described it as a 'violent political pamphlet' and it is true that it bore the marks both of haste and of bias. None the less it did the work it set out to do: it revealed a situation which could be allowed to continue no longer. It showed no more and no less than the 'complete breakdown of administrative efficiency, joined with a decay of the elementary rules of self-government'.[25]

The most frequent indictment made by the commissioners was the general loss of faith in the borough magistracy. In their

178

conclusion they spoke of 'a distrust of the Municipal Magistracy, tainting with suspicion the local administration of justice, and often accompanied with contempt of the persons by whom the law is administered.' [26] The same point was made time and time again as they visited successive towns. At Walsall the commissioner said that the conduct of the magistrates had undermined the confidence of the people in their justice and impartiality. In some places, such as Leicester, this distrust was definitely political in character. 'From a remote period there has existed among the inhabitants a widely spread . . . suspicion of the integrity of the magistrates in cases where political opponents are concerned, especially in cases of a political complexion.' [27] But underlying this, in whatever form it manifested itself, was the fact that by their oligarchical exclusiveness the borough magistrates had drawn apart from the communities which they were trying to govern. 'Hence, even in those cases in which injustice is not absolutely committed, a strong suspicion of it is excited, and the local tribunals cease to inspire respect. The corporate magistrates, generally speaking, are not looked upon by the inhabitants with favour or respect, and are often regarded with positive distrust and dislike.' [28]

The Act as it was finally passed in 1835 went to the roots of this corruption 'by two cuts of the healing knife of reform', as Redlich and Hirst have put it.[29] First, the office of magistrate was severed from corporate office: after 1835 the borough Bench was appointed by the same authority as the county Bench, the Lord Chancellor, and the only relic left of the old system was that the mayor remained ex officio J.P. and chairman of the Bench. Secondly, all administrative work was removed from the borough magistrates and handed over to elected town councils, with the exception of one or two matters such as licensing which were regarded as quasi-judicial. The appointment of a Justices' clerk was made compulsory, and his qualifications specified. Stipendiary magistrates, salaried police magistrates, might be appointed by borough councils on petition to the Secretary of State. In fact, since these were only permissive, in practice no more than twenty towns took advantage of them. There was still no general uniformity, but a hierarchy which ranged from the

Quarter Sessions boroughs which were for all practical purposes exempt from the jurisdiction of the county Justices, to those inferior boroughs which might or might not possess their own commission and were subject to the appellate jurisdiction of the county Bench.

The importance of the Municipal Reform Act lay far beyond its immediate achievement in establishing for the nineteenth-century towns an efficient and workable system of local government. It had in fact, though it was to take three generations or so for this to be recognized, established the principles which were ultimately to be extended to the county Benches as well. First, the separation of judicial and administrative functions; secondly, the introduction of representative institutions. ' "Local government had been municipalized" is the formula under which Englishmen summarize the history of the legislation which has ended in County, District and Parish Councils.'[30]

References

1. F. W. Maitland, *Township and Borough*, Cambridge University Press, 1898, p. 68, quoted W. S. Holdsworth, introduction to E. G. Dowdell, *A Hundred Years of Quarter Sessions*, Cambridge University Press, 1932, p. xlvii.
2. Levi Fox, *Stratford-on-Avon*, Jarrold, Norwich, 1953, pp. 98–100.
3. S. and B. Webb, *English Local Government: The Manor and the Borough*, 2 vols., Longmans, 1924, p. 367.
4. F. Hill, *Tudor and Stuart Lincoln*, Cambridge University Press, 1956, pp. 188–9.
5. The clause is actually taken from a charter of Winchester in 1587. T. Atkinson, *Elizabethan Winchester*, Faber, 1963, p. 153.
6. E. J. Homeshaw, *The Corporation of the Borough and Foreign of Walsall*, Walsall, 1960, p. 50.
7. Rev. J. Hodgson, *History of Northumberland*, 1832, pt II, vol. II, p. 429.
8. A. Temple Patterson, *A History of Southampton 1700–1914*, I, *An Oligarchy in Decline 1700–1835*, Southampton Record Series, Southampton University Press, 1966, p. 18.
9. C. Stella Davies, *History of Macclesfield*, Manchester University Press, 1961, p. 82.
10. Homeshaw, *op. cit.*, pp. 91–2.
11. Temple Patterson, *op. cit.*, p. 15.
12. Webbs, *op. cit.*, pp. 223–31.
13. Homeshaw, *op. cit.*, p. 83.

14. L. J. Ashford, *The History of the Borough of High Wycombe from its Origins to 1880*, Routledge, 1960, p. 231.
15. It is only fair to point out that in this particular instance it came to life again at the turn of the century. *ibid.*, p. 238.
16. Quoted Asa Briggs, *The Age of Improvement*, Longmans, 1959, p. 44.
17. Temple Patterson, *op. cit.*, p. 23.
18. But see the important article by E. P. Hennock, 'Urban Sanitary Reform a Generation before Chadwick', *Economic History Review*, 1957, x, pp. 113–21.
19. Quoted in E. P. Thompson, *The Making of the English Working Class*, Gollancz, 1963, p. 150 (Penguin Books, 1968).
20. A. Temple Patterson, *Radical Leicester*, Leicester University Press, 1954, p. 25.
21. *ibid.*, p. 24.
22. Webbs, *op. cit.*, pp. 697–8.
23. S. and B. Webb, *The Parish and the County*, 1906, p. 83.
24. Ten Bristol merchants sat on the Gloucestershire Bench at the end of the eighteenth century. See page 84 above.
25. J. Redlich and F. W. Hirst, *Local Government in England*, Macmillan, 1903, i, p. 116.
26. Report of the Commission on Municipal Corporations, Parliamentary Papers, 1835, xxiii, p. 112.
27. Temple Patterson, *Radical Leicester*, p. 208.
28. Parliamentary Papers, 1835, xxiii, p. 89.
29. *op. cit.*, p. 410.
30. *ibid.*, p. 128.

CHAPTER EIGHT

The Bench in the Twentieth Century

'THE prototype for a local authority in the nineteenth century was urban, but the Quarter Sessions continued to enjoy greater social prestige.'[1] The County Councils Act of 1888 did not alter this situation as much as might have been expected, or in some cases hoped. The county authority was now at last placed on the same footing as all the other public bodies which had been made open to election during the nineteenth century. The first elections in 1889 provided an opportunity for everyone to recognize the extent of the social changes which had taken place during the past fifty years, but on the whole the one thing that was apparent was that there was *no* immediate evidence of change. New County Council bore a face familiar from old Quarter Sessions. The *Devon Weekly Times* complained after the first meeting of the provisional County Council in January 1889 that 'the gathering looked much like Quarter Sessions . . . landlordism and squire-archy were in conspicuous force'.[2] When the first County Council proper met in April 1889 sixty-five of its 104 members were magistrates: nearly all the prominent members of Quarter Sessions were back again, and the few absentees were co-opted as aldermen. The familiar faces reappeared because social standing was still the accepted criterion for public service. The history of the magistracy in the twentieth century shows the slow, sometimes the reluctant, acceptance of the idea of professional qualification for the Bench. Still in the opening years of the century, certainly up to the outbreak of the First World War, the county Bench reflected county society, as it had always done. What differences there were are to be accounted for by the changes which were coming over county society itself during these years.

Local landed society continued to recruit new blood into its ranks, a process familiar enough in English social development, though probably the speed of incorporation had never been as quick as it was now. The merging of business and landed interests had become a two-way movement. On the one hand successful industrialists and company directors bought their estates and learned the manners of the country gentry; on the other hand farmers and landowners took every opportunity of investing in commercial enterprise, particularly in putting their money into urban property. Improved facilities for travel encouraged the flight from the towns, and a new class of people began to build themselves large neo-Gothic or neo-Tudor houses and enjoy the pleasures of country living without having to acquire enormous mansions with acres of parkland. The newcomers found that social acceptance was easier now than it had ever been before. Success at shooting or on the hunting-field of course would help considerably, as it had always done, and soldiering, like sport, gave a common standard of manners. Many men made the right sort of friendships and connexions through the camps and exercises of the Volunteer movement. Freemasonry also provided another important means by which a man might quickly and easily have the sense of belonging to a county, provided that he gained entry to one of the numerous masonic lodges which were springing up at this time. And then the public schools certainly played their part in standardizing upper-class manners, enabling the sons of businessmen and industrialists to acquire the ease of manner and the social familiarity which would carry them into the ranks of the established landowning families.

As a result the county Bench at the beginning of the twentieth century was less exclusive than before, recruited on a broader basis and containing a great cross-section of different interests. Among the Justices of the Peace for Cheshire at this time there were certainly a number of names from the old county families, but also included are Thomas Brocklebank, a Liverpool banker and shipowner; J. S. Harmood Banner, a Liverpool accountant and chairman of an iron company; W. L. Chew, a Manchester solicitor; William Laird, the Birkenhead shipbuilder; John Brunner, the alkali manufacturer. As J. M. Lee points out, 'the Duke of Westminster, who as lord-lieutenant was choosing magistrates from various positions in society, knew that government by landowners alone was no longer possible'.[3]

Appointment to the county Bench still in fact amounted to nomination by the Lord Lieutenant, since the Lord Chancellor merely confirmed his recommendations. In the boroughs the Chancellor nominated the Benches, exercising his powers in consultation with the local councils and others interested, such as the local M.P.s. By the end of the nineteenth century there was a growing unrest with the situation in the counties. Most Lord Lieutenants were of course politically active peers, but as long as both parties had a fair chance of representation, and while the landowning class reigned supreme, the position was accepted without question. After the Home Rule crisis of 1886 however the Liberals began to lose the support of the landowners until by 1892 only three Lord Lieutenants remained to support Gladstone in the Lords and it was estimated that only a very small proportion of the Justices were Gladstonians. There was therefore great pressure from inside the party to redress the balance, and the Lord Chancellor, Lord Herschell, did in fact make appointments to the Bench other than those recommended to him. But with the fall of the Liberals in 1895 and the return of the Conservatives the former practice was revived. When the Liberals returned to power in 1906 there was considerable agitation for further reform with regard to the methods of appointment. H. C. F. Luttrell, the M.P. for Tavistock, tried to introduce election and wanted the transfer of the powers of the Lord Lieutenants to municipal and county councils, proposals which he embodied in two private member's bills in 1907 and 1909 but which came to nothing.

The reform, when it did finally come, was introduced in 1910–11 by the Lord Chancellor, Lord Loreburn, in most unusual circumstances. With the support of the Prime Minister, Lord Asquith, who thought it worth while giving the system a trial before having it debated, he put into practice the recommendations of a Royal Commission. He introduced no very drastic change: he simply accepted the existing situation, but tried to improve the Lord Chancellor's information service. Lord Loreburn had already discussed the advantages of local committees before the House of Lords in April 1907, and had encouraged the Lord Lieutenant of Devon to form such a committee in the

December of that year – the first advisory committee with an official blessing. By the end of 1911 the majority of counties had established committees consisting of five or six members appointed by the Lord Lieutenant, who was not necessarily included himself. Their purpose was to advise him and it was then his duty to forward these recommendations to the Lord Chancellor. If the Lord Lieutenant should prove uncooperative the committee might bypass him and make direct approaches to the Lord Chancellor over his head.[4] The only important change since 1911 that was introduced by Lord Chancellor Cave in 1925, which ordered the appointment of members of these advisory committees for six years instead of for life, so that half the committee should retire in rotation every three years.

The present system is based on the recommendations of the Royal Commission on Justices of the Peace which was appointed in 1946 and whose report was published in 1948. There is a separate advisory committee for each area which has its own commission of the peace. The membership and the proceedings of these committees remain strictly confidential, though this tradition was broken in July 1967 when Lord Denning, Master of the Rolls, announced the names of the seventeen members of the advisory committee which recommends appointments in the Inner London area. Lord Gardiner, the Lord Chancellor, has said that in country areas where everyone knows everyone else, the local committees fear that if the names of their members were known 'they would be lobbied to death'. A pamphlet on the appointment of J.P.s issued in the summer of 1967 on behalf of the Lord Chancellor says that members of the advisory committees 'are drawn from all sections of the local community. Their identity is not disclosed in order that they may be shielded from undesirable and unwanted influences in performing their duties.'[5] The name and address of the secretary of each committee is however obtainable from the clerk of the County Council or from any clerk to the Justices. Many people of their own initiative present themselves for consideration, and voluntary bodies such as the British Legion, the Women's Institute or any political party may send forward names of people whom they consider suitable. Some advisory committees interview prospective candidates. 'I am under no obligation to accept their recommendations,' Lord Dilhorne told the Magistrates' Association in 1963 when discussing the role of the Lord Chancellor in regard to these advisory committees, 'and sometimes I decide to reject them if it does not appear to me that the candidate is sufficiently qualified, and sometimes I ask them to put forward other candidates.' It is scarcely surprising in the circumstances that many newly appointed magistrates feel that the machinery responsible for his or her selection is cloaked in mystery. 'He has had his greatness thrust upon him,' as one new Justice, who was sufficiently honest to express his bewilderment openly, put it.[6] Many feel it is a pity that this aura of mystery should remain and that it adds little to the dignity of the office.

The Royal Commission on Justices of the Peace in 1910 insisted that 'the benches were open to men of every shadow of political opinion and of every religious faith' and emphasized the need to remove 'political opinions and political action' from the influences affecting the selection of magistrates. This was echoed by the Royal Commission of 1948 which in its majority report accepted the consequences of committing the nomination of magistrates to party representatives, though the minority report, which included among its signatories Lord Merthyr, the chairman of the commission, urged that political nominations should not be considered for the Bench at all, and called for independent advisory committees and independent magistrates 'drawn from every social class whose qualifications are confined to character, intelligence and local knowledge'. The ideal of the non-political Bench is often raised. A leader in *The Times* commenting on a directive of the Lord Chancellor to advisory committees in November 1966 stated quite categorically that to take political affiliations into consideration in the making of appointments 'can in no way be conducive to the administration of good justice. . . . It would be a salutary further step forward if in future magistrates could be selected not in aid of any political balance upon the Bench but mainly upon their capacities for judgement.' But the policy of the Lord Chancellor is to preserve a balance of parties on the Bench so that all viewpoints are represented. This is the reason for the long-standing practice of asking all potential magistrates what party if any they belong to, a question which may at first sight be misunderstood, but which is intended to prevent the dominance of any single Bench by magistrates of only one political outlook. The directive mentioned above states this purpose clearly. 'The Lord Chancellor cannot disregard political affiliations in making appointments, not because the politics of an individual are a qualification or a disqualification for appointment, but because it is important that justices should be drawn and should be known to be drawn from all sections of the community and should represent all shades of opinion.'

'Politics on the Bench' always, of course, makes a good headline in the press, but the real point at issue is political bias after appointment, which is a very different matter indeed, and the accusations of this are mostly unfounded. Once a magistrate is appointed he is governed by his oath to 'do right to all manner of people after the law and usages of the realm without fear or favour, affection or illwill'. Justices with many years' experience on the Bench say that they are generally quite unaware of the party affiliations of their colleagues. It is in order to foster this state of affairs that the present Lord Chancellor has suggested that only a small proportion of new appointments should be local authority members.

One of the first actions of the Liberals on their return to power in 1906 was to abolish the property qualification for J.P.s. In 1918 women became eligible to serve as magistrates. In theory therefore the Bench is now open to all. In many of the larger industrial towns wage-earners are fairly represented, in some cases they even constitute a majority of the Bench, and large employers, such as the Coal Board or Boots, make it easy for their members to act as magistrates. But appeals are still made at fairly frequent intervals to employers to give their employees time, which generally amounts to twenty-six days in a year, to do this. Lord Denning commented recently on the applications made for the vacancies in the Inner London area that these still tended to come from a limited number of sources. For the office today remains one which requires leisure, or at least a considerable freedom from office hours, and which carries with it no financial remuneration. Subsistence allowances are not high, and are in any case not paid to anyone living within three miles of the court, a hardship which will be remedied, the Lord Chancellor announced in November 1966, 'when economic conditions allow'. According to the Justices' Allowances Regulations 1965 those who qualify are entitled to remuneration on a scale which ranges from 12s. 6d. for absence from home for four to eight hours, to £2 for more than sixteen hours' absence. The present government intends to introduce legislation to give J.P.s loss allowances similar to those now given to councillors, a move which would certainly help wage-earners to become Justices.

About a thousand new appointments of men and women are made every year to the commission of the peace. Despite its financial disadvantages the office remains exceedingly popular and the applications nearly always outnumber the vacancies. In the Inner London area for example there are between ten and fifteen applicants for each of the twenty vacancies which have to be filled annually. The usual number of magistrates sitting on the Bench is three, or at the most five. There is general agreement that the size of the Benches should be kept to a minimum. This small number is found to be the best for consultation: otherwise the public witnesses the not very dignified spectacle of magistrates whispering among themselves or of needing frequently to retire. In order that the individual magistrates shall get sufficient experience the rule is applied by the Lord Chancellor that a Bench which sits once a fortnight or less often should not have more than seven Justices; one which sits once a week should have a maximum of fourteen.

A gradual reduction in the retiring age of magistrates is at present under consideration by the Lord Chancellor. By new rules which came into force in October 1967, no one may be elected chairman of the Bench after the age of seventy, though probably the existing chairman if re-elected will be allowed to continue in office. The only age condition at the moment is that a new magistrate shall not be over the age of sixty at the time of his appointment. Only a quarter of the present magistrates are under fifty although, as the present Lord Chancellor has said, it is desirable that all Benches should contain a proportion of younger magistrates, men and women in their thirties and forties. The proposal to abolish *ex officio* Justices is one of the most important recent changes affecting the character of the Bench for this will eliminate approximately 1,600 mayors of boroughs and chairmen of County Councils, urban district councils and rural district councils who are Justices merely during their term of office.

1 January 1966 marked the end of the historic role of the Justice of the Peace as the untrained amateur. At last the Bench is coming into line with other spheres of government in accepting the need to be professional. The qualities which marked the amateur Justice are not however to be lost. The government says that the men and women appointed to the Bench are chosen for their 'commonsense, sympathy and wide experience of life and affairs'. In the old days a new magistrate might receive well-meant encouragement from his colleagues on the Bench: 'It's all a matter of commonsense of course.' Now it is accepted that commonsense is only the starting-point. Before he actually takes his seat on the Bench the intending Justice has undergone training in its widest sense. The Royal Commission on Justices in 1948 had recommended that new J.P.s should not sit until they had taken a prescribed training, but this had never been implemented. The Benches themselves had long been in favour of the idea, and the Magistrates' Association had been strongly pressing for it. The Association had in fact from 1949 published six lectures for magistrates which were intended for use by the clerk as the basis for training. About this time a number of university departments began providing courses for magistrates, either residential courses of a week, or a series of evening lectures run on extra-mural lines with each meeting consisting of equal periods of lectures and discussions. These courses were particularly valuable in providing exercises in sentencing where magistrates were divided into Benches and asked to adjudicate on fictitious cases.

The culmination of a movement which had been growing over the past twenty years in favour of introducing *compulsory* training for new magistrates came with the setting up in 1964 of the National Advisory Council for the Training of Magistrates, by Viscount Dilhorne, then Lord Chancellor, under the chairmanship of Judge C. D. Aarvold. The Advisory Council's advice to the Lord Chancellor formed the basis of the White Paper *The Training of Justices of the Peace in England and Wales* which was published in December 1965. Briefly the Paper, without requiring legislation, introduced a system of compulsory training for all new magistrates appointed after 1 January 1966. They have now to give an undertaking to complete a prescribed course of basic instruction within a year of their appointment, and if necessary to undergo a special course of instruction for juvenile courts either before election to a juvenile court panel or within a year afterwards.

The new magistrate is expected to attend court as an observer on at least three occasions for a total of at least six hours, to attend a series of elementary lectures on procedure from the clerk, and to do some required reading. When he has had some experience of the Bench he is ready to embark upon the second stage of the training, which must be completed within twelve months of his being sworn in. This covers in greater detail many of the matters dealt with earlier, rules of evidence, practice and procedure, the problems of punishment and treatment, probation and so on. It will also include visits to a prison and either a borstal or a senior remand home. The White Paper believes that it should be possible to complete this stage in a course extending over one week-end 'but two such week-ends would be preferable in order to allow more time for instruction and discussion'. The actual syllabus of the training is formulated by a committee of magistrates, and universities, particularly adult education departments, give advice and provide facilities.

Once he takes his seat on the Bench the new magistrate has the guidance of the magistrates' clerk, who is the duly appointed legal adviser to the Bench. It is assumed that most lay Justices will have little knowledge of the law and he is therefore always there to advise on matters of law and procedure, powers of sentencing and other similar matters. Most of the larger Benches now have a full-time clerk, who must by law be a barrister or a solicitor. 'The clerk who takes note of the evidence, the clerk who knows the law,' said Lord Denning, 'is the one sure adviser in the court on whom the laymen, with their inexperience, often rely with the utmost confidence and with the result that justice is done.'

In 1888 the County Councils took over roads, bridges and most other local responsibilities, with the exception of liquor licensing. At the same time the jurisdiction of magistrates was extended so that many serious offences formerly triable at Assizes were now dealt with by Quarter Sessions, while over the last fifty years the practice of summary jurisdiction has grown enormously. As a result the work which comes before the modern Justice of the Peace is as complex and as time-consuming, even if not as all-embracing, as that which faced his predecessors. Every year, according to a recent estimate, one in every forty persons in this country will appear before the magistrates.[7] Of the cases heard in the courts 97·5 per cent are dealt with by the lay magistracy. As in the past the only contact with justice for a massive proportion of the population will be with these amateur judges. 'The justice that matters most in the homes of the people is the justice that is administered by the magistrates on their Bench,' as the late Lord Merrivale recognized.

The work of Petty Sessions has increased so much because many of those whose offences are normally triable by jury take advantage of the option available to them to have their cases dealt with summarily by the Justices. In the counties the magistrates arrange petty sessional districts and hold a court in each district; in boroughs there is one courthouse and the magistrates will attend each court day by rota. Most of the offences created by the voluminous social legislation of the past fifty years are triable summarily, particularly offences against the traffic laws which now account for over half the convictions. (It should be pointed out however that all minor traffic offences may be dealt with in the absence of the accused, and this will generally be done although the accused has the right to appear if he wishes.) Though summary jurisdiction is mainly concerned with breaches of the criminal law a number of civil matters also come before the Justices, a fact which is not widely known, probably because they are immune from journalistic attention. Some of these, however, particularly cases arising from matrimonial disputes, are highly complex. This century has also witnessed another important development, the growth of specialized courts to deal with some particular aspect of the magistrates' work. An Act of 1908, often known as the 'children's charter', established the specialized juvenile courts. Since the Children and Young Persons Act of 1933 magistrates with special qualifications for the work are elected by their colleagues in each petty sessional division. They must be under the age of fifty on appointment and must retire at sixty-five. In London the juvenile court magistrates are nominated by the Lord Chancellor, but the proposal to extend this practice outside the metropolis was specifically rejected by the Committee on Young Offenders in 1927, and again by the Committee on Children and Young Persons in 1960. The practices and procedure of the London courts under such chairmen as Sir William Clarke Hall (1866–1922), however, have done much to shape the attitudes of the courts throughout the rest of the country, which deal with about 80 per cent of the juvenile offenders.[8] There are at present 820 juvenile courts in England and Wales (Scotland has never had very many), and out of an approximate total of 16,000 active lay magistrates in the country as a whole about 5,000 men and 3,000 women are members of juvenile courts. The fact that these magistrates also serve in the adult courts is valuable in ensuring a two-way flow of ideas. Juvenile courts have both a civil and a criminal jurisdiction, and there are provisions under the former for dealing with young people not as offenders but as being in need of care, protection or control.

Many criticisms have been made about the inadequacy of these courts to deal with the mounting tide of juvenile delinquency. Sometimes magistrates have been blamed unfairly, particularly in instances in which the relevant services are at fault, when for example remand homes or detention centres are full or psychiatric treatment is not available. There are undeniably certain weaknesses in the procedure, for instance the long delay which may occur between the commission of the crime and the time when the child is brought before the court. Any period of waiting will be long enough for the attitude of the parents to change from one of censure to one of protection and excuse for their child. It is also frequently suggested that in any case criminal proceedings are not suitable for dealing with children's offences and that a child of ten years (the age of criminal responsibility) can have little idea of such matters as the cross-examination of witnesses and the rules of evidence. But free legal aid is of course always available for the child and the responsibility is laid on the court in any case to see that his interests are looked after. The clerk, for example, will cross-examine witnesses on his behalf.

All courts are finding that the amount of work which comes before them is getting heavier each year. Crime increases steadily and relentlessly: former crime-waves fade into insignificance beside the unprecedented growth since the mid 1950s. One particularly serious aspect of this is that, just at the moment when criminal matters need to be sharply delineated, the issue of right and wrong is becoming blurred. The word 'criminal' has become so debased in its usage that it now covers every infringement of every regulation, whether the offender is morally to blame or not. One magistrate recently went so far as to say, in the pages of *The Magistrate*, that the failure to make a clear separation between criminal offences and innocent breaches of the law when dealing with offences against the Road Traffic Act 'is probably the major cause of the lack of confidence felt by so many people in the law, the magistracy, and the police, and indeed of the partial failure of the Act to achieve its purpose'. For motoring offences (including infringements of the speed limit) exceed all adult convictions for crimes of dishonesty and crimes against the person by approximately 50 per cent. The typical criminal of today is certainly not the thief, nor the thug who hits an old lady on the head to possess himself of her handbag or to ransack her house: the typical criminal of today is the motorist. Motorists constitute over 48 per cent of all those convicted of any criminal charge in any court. *In the eyes of the law* the guilty motorist is as much a criminal as the man who is charged with theft, assault or drunkenness. Yet the public emphatically refuses to recognize motoring offences as a crime, and no moral stigma attaches to the man who has failed to notice a road sign or left his car parked too long in a limited waiting area. As Barbara Wootton puts it, 'Apparently on the Marxian principle that the law is made and operated in the interests of the well-to-do, motoring offences generally, and infringements of speed limits in particular, are not ordinarily thought to "count" as crimes at all.' [9]

What is to be done about this? Lord Devlin suggested in an address at Birmingham University early in 1961 that real crimes should be tried by juries and punished by imprisonment, while quasi-crimes (offences which involved no moral wrong-doing but were mere disciplinary matters) should be tried by the magistracy and punishable by fines. The magistracy, he said, were particularly well qualified for this service since they were people strong enough to see the need for discipline themselves but as laymen ran no danger of getting out of touch with popular feeling. Yet the actual course of events today seems to be going in the opposite direction. Many sentences of imprisonment are imposed in magistrates' courts, and one of the suggestions of the Streatfeild Report was to add more offences to the list of indictable crimes. Motoring offences pinpoint the quandary: while the errant motorist is regarded as a criminal there can only be confusion in the public mind about the seriousness of crime in general. Lord Devlin propounded a solution for this problem which might find favour among Justices who have a large proportion of their time taken up with motoring offences: it is that the motorist should be regarded as a licensee who holds his licence during good behaviour. Magistrates are used to acting as a licensing authority: why should they not be custodians of good behaviour on the roads as much as they are of good behaviour in the public houses? Disqualification is the true and logical penalty of the careless and inefficient licensee: imprisonment is not. Yet in the interests of public safety there must be some ultimate sanction for persistent driving while disqualified or persistent refusal to pay a fine. There was general public outcry in February 1967 when an expectant mother was sentenced to three months' imprisonment for driving while disqualified. Yet the sentence was upheld, though reduced, by the Court of Appeal.

'A very fierce light beats upon the Magistrates' Courts,' as Lord Atkin said, and in many instances this is an excellent thing. Perhaps one aspect of the work of the courts which the press seizes upon more readily than any other is the question of disparity in sentencing. Thus a recent newspaper article drew attention to the case of two young men caught exceeding the speed limit in a built-up area by driving at seventy miles an hour. The first was fined £20, the second, a week later, £4. 'A contrast of that sort reduces justice to the level of a lucky dip,' commented the leader writer. But this is scarcely fair. Because an offence is the same, journalists, and thus of course their readers, judge that the cases must be similar. But they cannot be in full possession of the highly relevant background information which influences a sentence: the number of previous convictions, the man's financial situation, and the general circumstances surrounding the case. For the present position allows the court to have regard to aggravating or mitigating circumstances, and enables magistrates in fact to make the punishment fit the crime through the exercise of their discretion. Moreover a sentence given in a court is not given by the magistrates on their own. They can, and frequently do, ask for a case to be remanded to get a report from the relevant agencies, psychiatric, probation and so on. In a juvenile court magistrates cannot by law deal with serious cases without a school report and a report on home surroundings.

Most motoring offences receive uniform treatment. Some sessional divisions publish a *Guide to Penalties* so that there may be uniformity within the division. In any case this is the most promising field for rationalization and a standard scale of penalties for these offences makes good sense. But it is doubtful whether it is possible or advisable to extend the practice into other areas of magisterial activity. An attempt should certainly be made to end the worst sorts of inequality in sentencing. A study published in 1962 by a member of the Criminal Research Unit at the London School of Economics showed that during a four-year period the proportion of men over twenty-one found guilty of indictable offences and imprisoned by any one court ranged from 3 to 55 per cent.[10] Admittedly these were the extremes: in fact 60 per cent of all the courts had an imprisonment rate of from 14 to 28 per cent, and since meetings for sentencing exercises between the local Benches are now quite common such extremes are only likely to occur on the small and isolated Benches. There will of course always be differences: so much is inevitable as long as views differ on morality, responsibility, deterrence and so on. Often this flexibility is recognized and appreciated by the public. There are situations in which if certain facts are established the magistrates have little or no discretion, as for instance in enforcing payment of arrears of rent or ordering a tenant to quit after proper notice has been given. But this rigidity also leads to protests in the press. Under the heading 'eviction by sausage machine' one leader writer gave vent to his feelings of 'disgust . . . to find that the magistrates had no power to be merciful'.[11]

Any account of the magistracy today cannot be concluded without a brief mention of the peculiar position of London. Here an anomalous situation, in which two concurrent systems of criminal jurisdiction existed side by side, is at last being ended. It originated, quite unintentionally, in the Middlesex Justices Act of 1792 which set up seven public courts in various parts of London, similar to that already existing at Bow Street, with three Justices and their clerks who all received annual salaries and were compelled to pay their fines and fees to a Receiver accountable to the Treasury. The unpaid Justices continued to help at these courts but before long the professional magistrates were attracting most of the business and the lay magistrates found themselves dealing only with licensing, rate summonses and offences under various Acts where no fees were charged. Criticism of this state of affairs was voiced from time to time and in 1937 the Maxwell Commission recommended that lay Justices and metropolitan magistrates should be housed in the same building. Nothing however was done because of the outbreak of war and in 1949 the Justices of the Peace Act gave the Home Secretary power to specify the classes of case which lay Justices might deal with outside the metropolitan magistrates' courts. Since then they have had jurisdiction over a great variety of offences, particularly parking offences under the parking meter system. As well as this increase of jurisdiction in their own courts they have become more closely associated with the stipendiary magistrates. Since 1933, for example, there has been a panel of lay Justices to sit in juvenile courts, and from the 1950s they have been hearing cases from the stipendiaries' heavy lists in metropolitan courts whose accommodation makes this possible. Plans are in hand for more court buildings in the metropolitan area. But the real advance lies in the proposal, made by the Aarvold Departmental Committee in 1962, to integrate the two systems. When the Administration of Justice Act 1964 became law lay Justices and stipendiary magistrates in inner London became part of a single system of courts under the control of a committee equally representative of both. Two Justices will have the power of one stipendiary and the committee will decide how the work is to be divided.

Consideration of the present position in London raises the most fundamental question which can be asked about the whole system of Justices of the Peace in this country today: are the right people being chosen to serve on the Bench? Is justice being done on all Benches? Is it in fact time to abandon the lay Justice and to substitute the stipendiary? There would undoubtedly be strong opposition to the introduction of stipendiary magistrates as placing the freedom of the individual in the hands of one man without the safeguards of either a jury or a three-man magisterial Bench. There is also the practical difficulty of the Lord Chancellor finding enough professional lawyers to act as stipendiaries. And then who would pay for them? But a compromise solution might be possible. Could not a stipendiary serve each court flanked by two lay Justices? This would at once solve the problem of the amateurism of the Justices while preserving those distinctive qualities of experience and common sense which the English Justices of the Peace have brought to their tasks for the past six hundred years.

References

1. J. M. Lee, *Social Leaders and Public Persons. A Study of County Government in Cheshire since 1888*, Oxford University Press, 1963, p. 46.
2. W. G. Hoskins, *Devon*, Collins, 1954, p. 194.
3. Lee, *op. cit.*, p. 31.
4. On this see J. M. Lee, 'Parliament and the Appointment of Magistrates', *The Magistrate*, March 1961, vol. XVII, No. 3, pp. 40–43; April 1961, vol. XVII, No. 4, pp. 58–9.
5. *The Appointment and Duties of Justices of the Peace in England and Wales*, pamphlet prepared by the Central Office of Information on

behalf of the Lord Chancellor and the Chancellor of the Duchy of Lancaster, 1967.

6. *The Magistrate*, November 1958, vol. xiv, No. 11.

7. *Sunday Times*, 21 November 1965.

8. See Mrs W. E. Cavanagh, 'The Development of the English Juvenile Court', *The Magistrate*, June 1966, vol. xxiii, No. 6.

9. Barbara Wootton, *Social Science and Social Pathology*, Allen & Unwin, 1959, p. 28.

10. Roger Hood, *Sentencing in Magistrates' Courts – a Study in Variations of Policy*, Stevens, 1962.

11. *Barrow News*, 22 January 1965, quoted A. J. Brayshaw, 'An Occupational Risk or Hazard', *The Magistrate*, April 1965, vol. xxi, No. 4.

12. Mrs Barbara Gray, 'Reflections on the Recommendations of the Longford Committee', *The Magistrate*, June 1965, vol. xxi, No. 6.

NOTES ON FURTHER READING

I. General Studies of the Justice of the Peace

S. and B. Webb, *English Local Government: The Parish and the County*, Longmans, 1906, remains the essential work on the subject, monumental and authoritative.

B. Putnam, *Proceedings before the Justices of the Peace in the Fourteenth and Fifteenth Centuries, Edward III to Richard III*, Ames Foundation Publication, Cambridge, Massachusetts, 1938, has an introduction that is indispensable to anyone concerned with the medieval J.P.

C. A. Beard, *Office of the Justice of the Peace in England*, New York, 1904, though dated, can still serve as a good general introduction.

Bertram Osborne, *Justices of the Peace 1361–1848*, Sedgehill Press, Shaftesbury, 1960, is a mine of antiquarian information with little attempt to discuss or interpret the development of the magistracy.

A. L. Rowse, *The England of Elizabeth*, Macmillan, 1950, Chapter VIII, brings the Tudor Justice to life with a wealth of vivid detail.

Esther Moir, 'Sir George Onesiphoru s Paul', *Gloucestershire Studies*, ed. H. P. R. Finberg, Leicester University Press, 1957, is a study of a typical reforming eighteenth-century J.P. based on his own personal papers.

II. County Studies

Victoria County History of Wiltshire, University of London, Institute of Historical Research, 1957, v, is a most useful survey of the Justices in one county from the sixteenth to the twentieth century which incorporates all the most recent work on the subject. It is divided into three sections: J. Hurstfield, 'County Government 1530–1660'; W. R. Ward, 'County Government 1660–1835'; R. A. Lewis, 'County Government since 1835'.

A. H. A. Hamilton, *Quarter Sessions from Queen Elizabeth to Queen Anne*, Sampson Low, 1878. This is a pioneer work on the J.P.s drawn from local sources, mainly Devonshire records.

W. B Willcox, *Gloucestershire 1590–1640*, New Haven, 1940, is a useful study, particularly of the subordinates of the Justices.

T. G. Barnes, *Somerset 1625–1640*, Harvard, Oxford University Press, 1961, is especially valuable for its discussion of the relation s of local and central government during the years of 'personal rule'.

Eleanor Trotter, *Seventeenth Century Life in the Country Parish, with special reference to Local Government*, Cambridge University Press, 1919, is based on the Quarter Sessions records of the North Riding of Yorkshire.

M. G. Gretton, *Oxfordshire Justices in the Seventeenth Century*, Oxford Record Society, 1934, is a useful survey.

E. G. Dowdell, *A Hundred Years of Quarter Sessions: the Government of*

Middlesex from 1660 to 1760, Cambridge University Press, 1932, is interesting in dealing with the county magistracy in an urban situation.

J. D. Chambers, *Nottinghamshire in the Eighteenth Century*, 1932, 2nd edn, Cass, 1966, has a chapter on the county under the squirearchy which is not altogether favourable to the Bench.

Esther Moir, *Local Government in Gloucestershire, 1775–1800, A Study of the Justices of the Peace*, Bristol and Gloucestershire Archaeological Society Records Series, 1969, analyses the membership of the Bench, and shows in detail the Justices at work.

P. Styles, *Development of County Administration in the late XVIIIth and early XIXth centuries, illustrated by the Records of the Warwickshire Court of Quarter Sessions 1773–1837*, Dugdale Society Occasional Papers, Oxford, 1934, shows a Bench reforming itself.

J. M. Lee, *Social Leaders and Public Persons. A Study of County Government in Cheshire since 1888*, Oxford University Press, 1963, is mainly concerned with the County Council but has incidentally many illuminating things to say about the magistracy during the later period.

A great number of counties are in the process of printing their Quarter Sessions records, and these vary enormously in value. *Warwickshire County Records*, eds. S. C. Ratcliff and H. C. Johnson (Stephens, Warwick), is among the best. Nine volumes have appeared so far covering the years 1625 to 1696, and the several introductions constitute a most useful study of the seventeenth-century J.P. *Minutes of Proceedings in Quarter Sessions held for the Parts of Kesteven in the County of Lincoln, 1674–1695*, ed. S. A. Peyton, Lincoln Record Society, xxv–xxvi, Lincoln, 1931, is also clear and informative.

III. *Other County Officials*

Lord Lieutenant

Gladys Scott Thompson, *Lords Lieutenants in the Sixteenth Century*, Longmans, 1923, remains the pioneer work on a much neglected official.

High Sheriff

C. H. Karraker, *The Seventeenth Century Sheriff: A Comparative Study of the Sheriff in England and the Chesapeake Colonies 1607–1689*, University of North Carolina, Chapel Hill, 1930, is both useful and unusual in being comparative.

Clerk of the Peace

H. C. Johnson, *The Origin and Office of the Clerk of the Peace*, reprint from *The Clerks of the Counties 1360–1960*, ed. Stephens, Society of Clerks, Shire Hall, Warwick, 1961, is the best general discussion of the office.

T. G. Barnes, *The Clerk of the Peace in Caroline Somerset*, Leicester University Occasional Papers, 1961, is a much more detailed study.

IV. *Judicial Work of the Justices*

W. S. Holdsworth, *A History of English Law*, Methuen, relevant volumes (volume IV 3rd edn, 1945, deals with the Tudor J.P.), is by no means as technical as the title might suggest. I t provides quite the clearest and best general survey of the judicial aspects of the J.P.'s work.

L. Radzinowicz, *History of the English Criminal Law*, 3 vols., Stevens, 1948, is a wide-ranging study of the eighteenth- and nineteenth-century criminal law, with much that is relevant to the Benches of the time.

S. and B. Webb, *English Prisons under Local Government*, Longmans, 1922, is useful and also provides the best general survey of the movement for prison reform.

What was involved in keeping the peace can only be fully appreciated when seen against the background of contemporary unrest discussed in the three following studies:

M. Beloff, *Public Order and Popular Disturbances 1660–1714*, Cass, Oxford, 1938.

F. O. Darvall, *Popular Disturbances and Public Order in Regency England*, Oxford University Press, 1934.

F. C. Mather, *Public Order in the Age of the Chartists*, Manchester University Press, 1959.

V. *Administrative Work of the Justices*

The Poor Law

S. and B. Webb, *English Poor Law History*, I, *The Old Poor Law*, Longmans, 1927, is still indispensable, if only for the vast amount of factual information.

E. M. Leonard, *The Early History of English Poor Relief*, Cambridge University Press, 1900, 2nd impression 1965, remains the basic handbook for the Tudor and Stuart period.

D. Marshall, *The English Poor in the Eighteenth Century*, Routledge, 1926, is a clear and readable account of later developments.

E. M. Hampson, *The Treatment of Poverty in Cambridgeshire 1597–1834*, Cambridge University Press, 1934, is an important regional study.

D. Roberts, *Victorian Origins of the British Welfare State*, Yale Historical Publications, 1960, deals with the Poor Law after 1834, and with nineteenth-century social administration in general, in a most valuable way.

Roads

S. and B. Webb, *English Local Government: The Story of the King's Highway*, Longmans, 1913, is the most comprehensive study of the subject.

VI. *The Borough Justices*

The borough Justices have been badly neglected by historians and the whole subject of the urban Bench is in urgent need of research. The only general account remains that by the Webbs, *English Local Government: The Manor and the Borough*, 2 vols., Longmans, 1924. Otherwise material has to be gleaned from the histories of individual towns: some of the more useful are mentioned in the footnotes to Chapter Seven.

VII. *The Magistracy Today*

Handbooks such as F. T. Giles, *The Magistrates' Courts*, Stevens, 1963, will give a technical legal outline of the present position. But the best insight into the magistracy today is to be found in the pages of *The Magistrate*, the journal of the Magistrates' Association, which discusses all the issues of interest to its members, particularly such controversial matters as training, reform of juvenile courts and so on.

INDEX

MORE ABOUT PENGUINS
AND PELICANS

Penguinews, which appears every month, contains details of all the new books issued by Penguins as they are published. From time to time it is supplemented by *Penguins in Print* – a complete list of all our available titles. (There are well over three thousand of these.)

A specimen copy of *Penguinews* will be sent to you free on request, and you can become a subscriber for the price of the postage – 4s. for a year's issues (including the complete lists). Just write to Dept EP, Penguin Books Ltd, Harmondsworth, Middlesex, enclosing a cheque or postal order, and your name will be added to the mailing list.

Another title in the British Institutions series is described overleaf.

Note: *Penguinews* and *Penguins in Print*
are not available in the U.S.A. or Canada

Also in the British Institutions series

THE UNIVERSITIES

V. H. GREEN

The universities have always played a vital role in British society, but in the last fifty years their importance has increased as dramatically as their numbers. The resulting changes – and the need to understand them – have been very much in Dr Green's mind in writing this book.

His text provides a much needed short history of the 'stone' universities – Scottish as well as English – from their medieval foundations to the present day: but he has concentrated equally on the development of the 'red-brick' and 'plate-glass' universities and on the present role of university education as a whole in British society.

By relating the present system to its history and to social conditions Dr Green has shed light both on the present and past relevance of Britain's universities to her overall development.